C000301083

Journey with Grace

Finding Freedom
Through a Transformed Life

SARAH M. GRACE

First published 2020 by Sarah Grace Publishing
an imprint of Malcolm Down Publishing Ltd
www.malcolmdown.co.uk

24 23 22 21 20   7 6 5 4 3 2 1

British Library Cataloguing in Publication Data

A catalogue record for this book is available from the British Library.

ISBN 978-1-912863-29-7

Unless otherwise indicated, Scripture quotations are taken from the Holy
Bible, New International Version (Anglicised edition). Copyright ©1979, 1984,
2011 by Biblica. Used by permission of Hodder and Stoughton Publishers, an
Hachette UK company. All rights reserved.
'NIV' is a registered trademark of Biblica UK trademark number 1448790.

Disclaimer

All the stories and people in this book are real, and those concerned have
given permission for me to share their journey. All are anonymous and names
have been changed where the people concerned would rather not be known.
Although some of the details of these personal journeys have been changed
to ensure confidentiality, they are nevertheless true reflections of valid, real-
life journeys we can all learn from.

Cover design by Esther Kotecha
Art direction by Sarah Grace

Interior design and typesetting by 2K/DENMARK
Set at 11 pts. in Grace Dyslexic designed by 2K/DENMARK

Printed in the UK

Dedication

I dedicate this book to my very awesome
grown-up children

—— Josh and Nicole ——

I love you both dearly more than you will ever
know and if this is the only chance to tell
you in print, it is the best reason to write this
book and makes it all worthwhile.

You inspire me and I have kept going because
of you. I thank God daily for gifting me with
you both and I hope that I can leave a positive
ripple in your lives today and always.

Big cheer for Charlie 'my furry rock' and
Bella 'my shadow' – embedded in our hearts.
Always patiently by my feet as I write.

Thanks and Acknowledgements

To so many people who have helped me along my journey, I can only hope I helped you in yours.

You are priceless, you know who you are and I hope that you know the part you have played, I truly thank you from the bottom of my heart. Please do keep journeying with me, taking care of you for me.

A special thank you to Malcolm for taking a chance on me working in a whole new sphere of life in the world of publishing that I knew nothing about five years ago. Helping me find my talents and helping me to use them to surprise us both! Having read this book four times over before finally making it to print, you deserve a medal as that's way harder than a marathon.

I am extremely thankful to Klaus and acknowledge our creative journey to produce this wonderful font 'Grace' that has already helped fellow dyslexics to read easier. Thank you for seeing me, hearing me and making my dream come true – it has been like all my Christmases coming at once! My real Santa!

To Joy Schaverien, my counselling supervisor, who has been so kind as to give me an incredible endorsement that made the hard work suddenly seem worth it. Your ongoing support with clients is invaluable and I appreciate you stepping out in writing your books that have changed many lives, including mine, and still ripples on though my work.

Michele Guinness for believing in me and for your voice in my head for two years of writing and planning this book. Your input has been invaluable to me and I hope we get to journey together again.

Emily Markwick for your staying power of working on the journal with me and your inner beautify that I have had the pleasure of seeing flourish since you were five years old. Now a university graduate, please keep flying high and remember I watch on so proudly.

Mal Corden, your encouragement has been more than you will realise. Championing me along the way, singing with me on occasions and making me laugh and cry at most of all of our meetings. Thank you for all you have imparted to help me take flight. You are still my favourite Carpool Karaoke!

A big thank you and consideration to Cameron Grants family for the permission of sharing your story, we can only hope that this helps others along the way.

Doug Murrey for your wonderful inspiration of 'Broken Pots' and allowing me to use it.

Jane Brocklehurst for permission to use your article on 'Fear of Success' from the ACW magazine.

Thank you to all the authors who have given me inspiration to write my own book. I am in awe of each and every one of you. Thank you for your gift of writing and expression that we may take for granted.

All of the published authors of Sarah Grace and Malcolm Down who are mentioned and for the ripple you created in my life as you were brave enough to introduce us to your ideas. Birthing these with you has been an incredibly interesting journey, each one different from the next. We keep on learning from you.

Especially:
Andrew Davies for your inner strength and determination.
Andrew McDonough in Australia who always makes life better somehow. Your ripple has travelled far, making creative and fun ripples in my direction for sure!
Caris Grimes for your gentleness and wisdom.
Emily Owen for the blessing you have always been to me since we met; you inspire me.
Mark Stibbe for such a life-changing redirection we have both been on!
Wendy H. Jones, knowing you and the journey creating Bertie will stay with me for my whole life (such fun!).

Thank you to all those who have written, or have allowed me to write their stories to share with you, especially Tony, Pat, Suzanne, Simon, Sally, Sarah, Helen and Beth.

Thank you to all my clients who have been brave enough to come to start unpacking their journey. For all those who have given permission to share their story.

Friends and family who have been there all along cheering me on from the side-lines just to survive let alone write a book. I couldn't have done this without you all – all different kinds of favour and blessings have come my way because of knowing you. I have learnt from each one of you and I hope I have blessed your lives in even a small way of being thanked.

You are immeasurable and irreplaceable. Thank you for loving me through the tough times and the good times – that's true love and blessing. I feel the favour in my life that is hard to put into words has come from God through you. Please stay on this journey we call life as I am rich for having you with me.

May I mention just a few:

John for believing me when I step out, for not believing me when I say I can't do it. Your support means more than you will ever know, you go far and beyond – thank you.

My brother Steven who has been there since day one and even though so far away I know you have my back. Thanks for always being there; I would have chosen you for my big brother.

Nessie Griggs (especially for helping me pack each time!), Cherri Heart, Lydia, Mark and Jake Faithfull, my Sue (Payne), Chris Novelli, Andy and Lindsay Rollett, Cameron Thorner, Caroline Ambrose, Caroline O'Farety, Ian Harvey, Wendy Howson for the injections of passion, just not enough time in this lifetime to cover all we want to – what a problem to have! Mark Helvadjian, my pastor who steadily steers our ship despite the storms; I hope we get to surf a few more spiritual waves in the future.

To all those gone home already who have taught me to love and keep loving, forgiving and learning; my mum especially, I miss you yet somehow you are still near in the small things, my handwriting and in my daft moments! You were a champion of the underdog and rose to the top – I just strive to be the best I can be, you did immeasurably more. Thank you for being you and your part in moulding me.

Endorsements

In this brave book Sarah Grace puts her life on the line in every sense. Woven throughout the book is the story her life's journey and its vicissitudes. Ultimately it is a tale of optimism, faith and of light coming out of darkness. The moving accounts of those she has met along the way, will inspire others to keep going through their bleakest times. Spiritual and emotionally engaging it bears witness to the ways in which hope and meaning may emerge where least expected.

Joy Schaverien PhD, Jungian psychoanalyst, author of *Boarding School Syndrome:The Psychological Trauma of the 'Privileged' Child* (Routledge) and *The Revealing Image: Analytical Art Psychotherapy in Theory and Practice* (Jessica Kingsley)

It's been said many times people relate more to your scars than your success stories, in this relatable, honest and vulnerable book Sarah tells us story with real authenticity.

Patrick Regan OBE,
Kintsugi Hope

Contents

Introduction

Creating a Contagious Ripple

Imagine your best friend was struggling and you knew they were near to death. What would you do?

'Anything imaginable; everything at all possible!' I would hope to hear your heart yelling at you.

As I was writing this book, a friend was suddenly in great need; her life fell apart around her. I was tested with regard to my own response as I felt her giving up and shutting down. I had to remember what it was like for me when my own life crashed and burnt before my eyes. What did I need then, and what would she need now?

Now imagine it's you . . . you are the one in need. Do you refuse offers of help and die quietly with no one around, like an injured animal, or do you reach out?

It's hard to know how we will react until we are in such circumstances, but for this point in time let's go with your initial thoughts.

Like I did, you would want to give your friend the best love, help and support in all the areas you could: physically, emotionally, spiritually and financially, wherever possible. Nothing held back; all out to change the outcome.

I am sorry for those for whom this will provoke a deep response, as there are very many sad stories of those who have lost loved ones and faced other crises, but do stay with me in this. I would like you to put yourself in that place now, yet the one you are being enabled to help is yourself. It doesn't mean you have to do it alone – absolutely not. No, we are about to journey together through thick and thin. In this book you will find the tools to help you do that as you dig deeper inside.

If we want to 'fill it, not feel it', we will lead ourselves into a self-fulfilling prophecy. We fill our time, our minds and our hearts with many things. This creates clutter – yes, even our hearts can become cluttered, divided and unsettled. We can become driven and seemingly do well. Yet being able to settle to one thing and be in the moment can be extremely difficult.

My hope is that this book will help you turn confusion into clarity, fear into peace, anxiety into creativity, doubt into trust. I hope it will give you confidence for your path ahead and freedom to live feeling fully alive and fully you. When we feel comfortable in our own skin, it is amazing how naturally contagious this is to others.

Taking time for ourselves is an acceptable thing to do these days, but we can still feel as though it is selfish and end up denying ourselves the time we really need. We may get to the gym and workout to improve our body, yet inside we are hurting and melting away emotionally.

As a psychotherapist, unpacking the journey and seeing what's really going on is something I am privileged to see many of my clients go through. Afraid of seeming self-centred, they sometimes say, 'But it's all about me – isn't that wrong?' So my question is, if you aren't going to do it for yourself, who will?

We can encourage others far more easily than go there ourselves. I have found, from talking with clients, that it echoes back at me, and I knew I needed time out to write this book. It took three years to get myself way from everything and settle for a week to write. Whether it would be published or not, I knew I had to make use of all the many moments I wanted to share. This was it; no one else could do it for me or make me do it; I had to go there myself.

I have been told I have a gift of encouraging, prompting and connecting people. Embracing this, along with a passion to help people to live a more fulfilled life, has led me to write this book, *Journey with Grace*. As a qualified and practising psychotherapist working also in publishing, I have had the privilege of encouraging and working with many different people. I will share some of these stories, mainly anonymously, to show how our ripple can be felt by others.

This book is for anyone who feels like they have worked hard to reach their goals and dreams, their job and family, yet are now feeling dissatisfied with life. Having gained life experience, relationships and adventures, our perception is that it should feel good, that we should be enjoying that feeling of wholeness inside when we think of our lives, enjoying every day because of the decisions we have made and because we have worked hard at it. We have invested in family life and kept the home fires burning while keeping a professional life going too.

Then bam! There it is!

We have arrived – yet we have a feeling of disillusionment that was never promised. Where do we go from here? Seek out pleasure in other relationships before the midlife crisis hits, or is that part of it?

So everything stops and we are forced to review our life.

As I am writing this book, the coronavirus has just hit our nation, and the whole world is changing before our eyes. We are experiencing the enforced shutdown of everything we know. What will help us hold on to hope, our nerve, our peace . . .? What have we invested in? Does it still give us all that we need to survive and will it allow us to thrive again?

I hope this book will help you see what you have inside already that has perhaps got lost somewhere along the way, or maybe this will be a little more finely tuned and can be 'regifted' back to you. This can then be passed on to others, especially to our younger generations, as we learn how to life our lives better.

What a privilege to get away to write, to leave everything behind. What a joy! Maybe your joy is not to write but to explore further emotional challenges. This writing did that for me as well. Whatever your journey needs to be, that will be the privilege, as no one needs it more than you.

My contact details are in the back of the book, so we can continue a professional healing journey going forward, if you wish to.

How to use this book

Journalling

Hopefully you have bought this book with the accompanying journal. If not, the journal is available to purchase on its own – or just grab a notebook.

I had the pleasure of working with the marvellous Emily Markwick on the design of the journal that accompanies this book. It was a dream for us both to work together and we have been so excited to see it come into being. I really hope you find pleasure in journalling as you read and work through this book.

There is something very powerful about seeing our thoughts on paper. It can help to make more sense of things. It is also good to hear ourselves say things out loud. During counselling sessions, I often hear both children and adults say things that seem to surprise them. This is a moment of recognising what is going on subconsciously. Journalling is a wonderfully private moment in which we can make further connections.

Any of my clients reading this will smile, I am sure, as I find it is one of my repeated phrases:

'Do you think you can write down what is coming up for you?'

I became fascinated with the idea of the journal as I saw how it linked with journey. Journey means 'to travel on a defined route', 'one's path in life'. It comes from the old French *journée*, meaning 'a day's length'.

The Vulgar Latin *diunum*, 'day', is a noun use of the neuter of Latin *diunum*, meaning 'of one day', which in turn comes from the PIE (Proto-Indo-European) root *dyeu* meaning 'to shine'.

I played with this in my mind for a while and realised that really we only have the day in which to shine, and then it dies. We do not get that chance again, but if we are fortunate enough to have another, and another, we can continue to shine each day. As we learn to live in the moment, feeling fully alive, we can learn from the day as it ends. As it dies, we can reflect on it, try to process it and learn from it. Another day comes . . . for some, although for some it ends, and there is no guarantee how many days we will get.

This has become a reality for many as we faced the coronavirus, and we have all recognised the stark truth of how vulnerable we are. No amount of money or status in society can keep us protected; we only have the day in which we live to be thankful for all we have.

It is hard to live as though we will not be alive tomorrow, as we live in a world of planning ahead. Yet there is tremendous value in being aware of and holding a moment in time that we can enjoy and treasure, even if it is not a huge moment. Seeing a feather float by or spotting a child playing in the leaves is a moment to hold on to.

Journalling is really helpful, even if it is sporadic; it can help us see things for what they are. As we journey on, it shows us how far we have come. In the difficult days it is easy to forget the good, and we often don't remember the wonderful things others say about us.

It is hard to get started sometimes, as it can feel like a chore, but even just writing some notes here and there will help to make sense of your thoughts along the way. Later, it becomes a wonderful gift to look back and see how far you have come.

I would recommend any men reading this to get hold of Patrick Regan's journal *This Is Me*, or another journal that feels comfortable to use.

Gracelets

'Gracelets' are gifts, like little gems, that I want to bring in bite-size portions. Each Gracelet is pulled from the preceding chapter and relates to that chapter's topic.

I hope these Gracelets will help you get your head around or encourage the spiritual part of your journey. Our spirit is there and present, whether we choose to acknowledge it or to ignore it. I see people who are in tune spiritually really shine; it is hard to ignore it. We can call it an aura, a glow, many different things, but it is evident even if the person themselves can't see it. It cannot be put on; it is the effect of feeling good spiritually, just like a person who is in love or pregnant will glow.

Just like this, we can feel loved and connected spiritually every day. In the same way, we can see the Holy Spirit shine through people when they are truly giving space to listen to God. I hope to be one of those people and to impart that to others; I really do not want to miss out on anything, and I don't want you to either.

Gracelets reflect all aspects of life that are explored in each chapter, not only the spiritual elements. So if this is an area that you are not fully comfortable with, don't worry – you will still gain much from working through the book.

Your Ripple

When we are further along this privileged journey, we can be there for others, really there in the moment, enjoying ourselves and others around us. Living the dream in our everyday life! The way to truly regift to another is to go to that deep place in in ourselves and find the gift within us, and then help others find theirs. I believe this is beyond coaching; it is going deep within ourselves and then coming out to give help to others. My journey has been this, and I am very willing to share it to help others move beyond fears to truly live freely as themselves, happy in their skin.

I have heard a number of great sermons by Mark Helvadjian, the minister at my church, who is a man who clearly listens to God. One Sunday, I thought to myself,
'He's really God driven,' and then he preached,
'Love propels you, whereas fear drives you.' Then I could see his love for God, his love for his family and his love for us as his church, modelling how this love was propelling him.

We need to check ourselves to see what is behind our actions and motives. If we are so busy being full of our own stuff without checking in from time to time, we may miss that we are finding it hard to hold anything of anyone else's. We are full to overflowing. Can you remember a time you have been really stressed? At such times we become selfish and self-centred while we resolve the issues; self-preservation kicks in. To stay in that place and not be able to see others is a sad and lonely ripple to create.

So at the end of each chapter, the section entitled 'Your Ripple' contains a number of questions. These can be used as a study guide for groups to work through each chapter together or you can work through them alone, with your journal.

Chapter 1

Unpacking the Journey

When I pack to go off on one of my adventures, I need to make sure I have unpacked from my previous travels. I really don't enjoy packing, let alone unpacking. But we have to start our journey with the unpacking first. In the same way, I just knew this book had to start with the unpacking.

We have all already packed without knowing it in our lives. Our bags are often full, and we often neglect to check what we might have picked up along the way. All our behaviour, thoughts and feelings affect us, and this ripples out to others. So let's look together at some of the things that we have unintentionally 'packed'.

My journey of life started a little shakily. Bringing me into this world was an incredibly strong woman who did not know how strong she was. My mum, Peggy, felt abandoned by my father because he left when I was only months old and my brother was two and had not yet learnt to walk. Even though she was unwell herself, she had no choice but to singlehandedly, yet wholeheartedly, look after my brother and me until she met our stepfather.

Being a mum myself and a psychotherapist, I now recognise that this stress led to ill health for my mum and also for me. We were both in and out of hospital, together and separately. I would have suffered separation anxiety.

My brother would have experienced the same, along with trauma as a result of being left at a young age without his mum and not knowing why. The effect of this time on us would have been profound, yet it was not talked about or explored. I had to do this in my own counselling sessions while I was training as a therapist, and it has opened my eyes and given me so much understanding of myself and how our early years affect us. We cannot change our beginning, but it helps to know what has happened to us. And we can change how we journey on – so all is not lost!

Within my counselling room the words began to take a similar path: 'unpacking' and 'journey' kept coming up. These words resonated both with my clients and with my own feelings of journeying with them. Each client takes me on another journey as I explore what is in the room and what stays with me after the sessions. I am learning from each client as each one is on a unique journey.

We can unknowingly continue on the same path time and time again. The same patterns emerge and we complain that things repeat themselves:

'Why am I here again, on this same mountain?!'

Sadly, most of us were not taught at school how to get to know ourselves or how to be in relationships. We have been influenced by the experiences of our early years, by our families and by things that have happened to us that have changed the way we view and relate to the world. These all bring about an effect on our own lives and others around us. We have been shaped by our parents, who in turn have been shaped by their parents, and so it goes on. Conversely, the lack of these – absent parents – will affect us dramatically too.

We can choose to repeat the pattern or, as often happens, we can do the opposite without much thought as to why we are doing it. So, for example, we may choose to have a small family because we grew up in a large one. Consciously or not, the lack of attention may well have left a strong feeling that we want to do things differently for our children.

Why Bother for Just One?

It takes a mix of courage and bravery to stop and look to why we do what we do.

You may ask:
'Why bother? Why not just get on with life?'
'Why should we do this? Nothing will change; it is what it is.'

Or maybe not . . . maybe it's the realisation that we *can* do something about it that threatens us the most. That we can see where we have been affected by our past even though we had not seen it before.

Knowing that we can unpack the past by stopping to see where we are can be the most privileged and empowering journey we will ever take. For me as a therapist, to journey with another is scary, exciting, challenging and fulfilling, and I wouldn't miss it for the world! That's why I have written this book – so that I can help others to stop for a while and look within themselves to make a difference going forward. Even if it only helps one, it will have been worth it, just like the story of the little boy on a beach who sees all the starfish that have been washed up. He starts to throw them back, one at a time. A man sees him and says to him,
'You can't make a difference; there are so many.'

The little boy says,

'But, sir, I made a difference for that one.'

And as he picked up another,

'And that one . . .'

We want our children to make good choices and not make the same mistakes. What if we can make a difference to them – even just one of them?

But we are still making the same mistakes. Why do we do this?

Helping ourselves is hard. We sometimes prefer to help others so that we can avoid looking at our own lives. So before we can help our children, we need to go there ourselves.

This struck me years ago as I travelled with my children on a long-haul flight to Australia. During the safety briefing, in the event of an emergency we were advised to put on our own oxygen mask before helping our children with theirs. I was uncertain whether my instinct to help them first would get the better of me. I found it challenging to sit and think about it as I looked at my children. Then I got my head around the reason for it and realised that surely this is what we should be doing in everyday life?

When we look deeper within, we are more able to give to others more wholly. I have seen bereaved clients who allow the feelings of loss in each phase of grief to surface, then they are able to start to help others. They can heal more wholly and bring about purpose and value. However, I have also had clients who have tried to skip this process and start trying to help others. This does not go so well.

The feelings get buried and then resurface later, creating relationship issues. Some experience another loss, and this complicates things even further. This is termed a 'complicated loss' and takes a highly qualified therapist to help work through the many layers.

Allowing time and space to be with our emotions and feelings is essential. This may relate to the loss of a loved one, of a job or of a lifestyle. Loss comes in so many forms that sometimes we find it hard to even identify something as loss.

Scattered Pearls

Unpacking our journey can be done at any time, but most clients come to see me at times of crisis. One client said, 'I've tried everything, and things keep going wrong.'

I have worked with many clients who have a similar fear to that which rose up in me during my training; the fear that it will all fall apart. One such client was struggling to find the words. I pulled up my sleeves, determined to help him find a way of expressing himself.

As I did so, a bracelet I was wearing broke, and the pearls scattered across the floor. I looked at the pearls all over the place and I said,
'Does it feel like this will happen to you, Simon?'

'That's it. That's exactly what it feels like. My fear is that I'll fall apart and not be able to pull it back.'

His sense was that letting go of his emotions would lead to falling apart and breaking down into many scattered pieces. Talking it out and seeing this symbolically untapped the deep trauma he would have experienced but had no memory of.

I reminded him that he had not fallen apart, even when it felt as though he would. Prior to having been adopted as a baby, Simon would have felt a desperation to have his needs met simply to survive, small and vulnerable. So, I remind him that he did survive then.

When he was older, he was sent away to boarding school. As he left all that was familiar, which had given him security, the same desperate feeling would have raised up in him even though he had no conscious memory of the initial pain. Again we revisit this with further understanding this pain and I remind him again he survived with the strong survival skills he had already developed to get this far.

I reminded him that he has support and love now; his wife, family and friends and this therapy. He has a deeper level of understanding of himself, as well as for his family and friends. He sat with this feeling and his understanding of it for a while, then in our next session he referred back to 'that moment' of my bracelet breaking, making it so visually clear. It was a powerful moment of seeing his internal pain.

Simon works with people with disabilities, helping them 'keep it together', so he has turned things around for good. His specific work is with vision loss, helping people to see more clearly and to manage more easily. He is on a journey himself to seeing more clearly. This link was so interesting; it was emotional yet rewarding.

I love those moments of breakthrough, and I love that I can be there to experience them with my clients.

Restoring a part that had been broken, helping someone feel a little more complete: to facilitate this is somewhat beyond words for me. We will often revisit these moments of breakthrough as they are so profound it takes a while to really consolidate how they have shaped life thereon.

When insecurity comes close to the surface, the original pain can feel as though it is real and present once again. Working on this together can help the client to recover more quickly each time. In the meantime, they are more self-aware, holding it in mind and know I am holding them in mind. This is what may have been missing or similar to a parent holding us always in mind.

Helping someone become more of a whole person and less of the broken child, enabling someone to develop maturity at no matter what age, is vital. It's a privilege to be with a client to enable them to really find complete understanding and acceptance of their past.

Threats and Challenges

We try to avoid things that threaten and challenge us. We can live in avoidance. Part of this is because we can be fearful of the unknown. We really do not know how we will respond to a particular situation. We might take a guess and say,

'Why did they do that? I wouldn't have done it that way.'
However we do not know what we don't know.

We are now living in very anxious and uncertain times. Since I started to write this, the world has changed before our eyes. In the first draft of this book, I wrote:

However, we actually do not know how we will react if we were to find ourselves in that situation for real; it is all speculation. We think we can decide how we are going to react to threats and challenges, yet most of the time we don't know how. We can only try to predict as we look at our own patterns of behaviour and know ourselves.

Now many of us are facing the most uncertain time of our lives, and we are beginning to see just how we would react. However, as I write, it is still early days, so we are still to discover the true and full effect of the times we are living in. It would be interesting to see whether you have reacted in a way you would have expected yourself to react to the changes in the way we are doing society, with the need for social distancing, the shutting down of businesses and the consequential loss of income and even of lives.

In 2019 I travelled to the USA for a week of writing at my friend's home in Richmond, Virginia. I was then going to travel on to Nashville for a publishing conference. This trip was going to be one of extremes: hiding out quietly, away from the heat, by a cool pool, writing and hoping that the manuscript for this book would fall into place; and then to a busy, cool, air-conditioned conference hall full of enthusiastic authors, suppliers, publishers. I hoped my trip would be fruitful and fun.

Travelling to the USA and trying to pass through security at the airport highlighted to me some of the threats we currently live with. Thousands of people were queuing and the computers were down.

Everyone was mumbling, feeling stressed and tired, as was I. The guards in the cubicles at security, who were not letting people through, became a potential threat to everyone, as people began to worry that they might miss their flight. I watched a scenario or two play out before me, as I had to queue for a good two and a half hours. Some people were edging towards those in front of them, even if there was no real movement forward of the queue. Psychologically, they needed to feel that they were getting somewhere in this painful experience.

I was watching one situation so intently that when the queue moved forward, I was oblivious to it. The situation before me involved Martin Clunes, a famous English actor. I fondly remember watching him in *Doc Martin*, with my family. As I watched the scene unfold at the airport, I was thinking,

'Well, we all know who he is, so why can't he just have his passport checked and then move along, rather than suffer this long wait with everyone, including me, watching him.'

Then a lady behind him, whom I initially thought was his wife, stumbled and fell backward.

'Why isn't she being taken care of, by him or by someone else?'
I thought. There was no reaction from Martin other than a brief glance.

'Gosh, I hope this isn't his wife.'
My thoughts were running all over the place.

Time passed, and we were all still there. No one seemed to have been set free over the border yet. The woman then fell forward and headbutted Martin in the back. He glanced back but kept very calm, as did his companion. In fact, he laughed at the whole scenario. By now he was next in line, so there was little risk of the headbutting happening again. I realised that the lady appeared to be drunk and could hardly stay upright. It also became clear that she was not his wife, nor did she have any connection with him at all, even though she had been standing so close to him she could easily have been assumed to be travelling with him.

The risk of this situation to Martin Clunes's reputation, and the risk for him of missing his connection or an event, may well have been on his mind. He turned to his companion, laughed, made a gesture of 'calm', and ran his hands downwards as if to create a calmness in his body. He was not immune to this situation because of who he was.

Even a recognisable celebrity had to go through the identification process: the whole finger, hand, thumb on both hands, photo and ticking of all the boxes to get into the country. There was no way around the security procedure, neither for Martin Clunes nor for the hundreds piling up behind him. We had all stepped out of our place of origin and into a new realm, so the process had to happen.

We can stay in our comfort zone and not venture out, and not know how much we will be missing out on. Martin Clunes could not control this process any more than I could. His status as a well-known performer made no difference: he also had to go through the uncomfortable process in order to get to his destination.

This is what it is like for us as we change our perspectives and move into new areas of understanding, whether it be emotionally, mentally, physically or spiritually.

It is like gaining access into a different country. We have to endure this part of the entry process. Hopefully we will get to enjoy the new country's greatest pleasures when we get through. Really there was no choice but to tolerate the process, unless we wanted to turn back. People only tend to get turned away if there is an issue, so the majority of the thousands do survive the process.

We can choose to go to the USA or any other country, to move out of our comfort zone, to encounter security, to face the threat of terrorists or the risk of being turned away. We have choices: the choice of whether or not to engage and the choice of how we handle it when we are there.

We might feel out of control too, at any point. The lady was no longer in full control of her body. Martin Clunes was clearly trying to stay in control of himself through the use of humour and calming exercises. The security officers were not shouting or getting obviously stressed as the queues grew in length and tension. I chose to watch these stories unfold, rather than get anxious about my connecting flight.

Curiosity Kills the Cat?

While on that USA trip, I stayed with my wonderful friend of many years, Cherri, who is well known for her love of cats. She had three gorgeous Ragdoll cats roaming the house as I was writing – Blue, Sky and Bump. They followed me around, intrigued to see what I was doing. This allowed them to learn that there were places within the house that they had not been to before. They are house cats, living in this beautiful big house in Virginia. They are very well taken care of, and within these boundaries they are incredibly safe.

Yet they saw more to explore as I opened doors and they peered in; it opened up their world, just like the border of the USA opened up to me, about to offer me the whole of a different country.

What is the risk to us of exploring further? Fear, disappointment, rejection, hopes being dashed, dreams not being realised, failure, excitement, achieving, joy, completion . . . the list goes on.

Listen to your own thought processes about the risks you face. These are the things that came up for me while I was writing this book:

- ▶ Will I miss something?
- ▶ Will I manage to achieve what I have set before myself?
- ▶ Will I get in my own way?
- ▶ Will something else get in my way, will I ever finish it?
- ▶ Maybe I can't do this and was never meant to.
- ▶ Was I just blowing this up in my mind to create importance for myself, a purpose and reason?
- ▶ Will anyone actually read it and benefit from it?

Take a few moments to think about some of these questions and how they apply to you. Write your thoughts and responses in your journal.

Safer to Keep Sleepwalking?

Hearing people voice their thoughts and helping them write these down on paper enables them to be understood and expanded: this is what I love to do to help people unpack their processes, unpack the journey.

I have had a number of clients who have said to me things like:

- 'I feel like I have sleepwalked though my whole life and my marriage.'
- 'What was going on for the last twenty years of my life? I don't think I was in it and can't remember it.'
- 'I was asleep at the wheel of my life and my marriage has crashed without me even realising.'

Such things are so sad to hear, yet these people are in my therapy room because they have recognised these issues now, which means they can start unpacking what's going on underneath. Knowing what we are really thinking and what's really going on is like the beautiful cat, Blue, finding a new room and going in with trepidation. Yet he now knows it's there, and he is intrigued. While he has the chance to get to it, he does. Something may startle him and he may run away, but he will be back because he knows it's there.

We can be like this as we get to know something new about ourselves, as we take a step forward towards a new part of our own world, be it internal or external. However, the internal can be more exciting and terrifying than travelling to new places with a visa across a border.

These are the kinds of thoughts that can start to grab us:

- What will I find?
- Will I like it?
- Will it be the undoing of me, like the bracelet?
- Or will it be the making of me?
- What if I have no purpose or special gift?
- Will I even like myself, or will others like me?

We are defending a huge amount of thoughts that we have collected over time. This is why the journey needs to be unpacked before we can go any further with our eyes wide open, not drunk like the lady in the queue. We are able to calm our minds down, like Martin Clunes, and know we are not travelling alone. We are able to travel ahead, like Blue and Sky, adventuring with caution into new places – and hopefully they won't get the better of us.

Hidden threats and challenges feel bigger when we do not deal with them. Like shadows or things niggling at the back of our minds, they just don't go away. Even practical things, like that tax return, filing or whatever it is we put off, will grow in size if left to its own devices. When something arrives, we can face it head on if we have cleared out the past and can start afresh from today.

Journal Your Journey

This book has become my journey for the last year: as I am writing I am pretty much living and reliving through all the areas I am writing about. It can be tough, yet it can be liberating.

What are the moments in your life that you love to treasure? I love it when I am stopped by people to admire my two Collies. I enjoy others enjoying them, and I like to be ready with my responses:

'Yes, they take a lot of grooming, and yes, they possibly are related!'

Put all these thoughts into your journal if you can.

Gracelets

The gems from this chapter I would like to shine through are how important it is to stop, to take a look at our past and to recognise how we got here. Our reaction to this in our everyday can be changed; we are not stuck here. We are not doing this alone, and the rest of the book will guide us along the way. We can't change our past, but we can change the way we allow it to mould our future.

Being curious about ourselves and others opens up our minds and allows others to do the same. Being curious is key; it holds back self-doubt, harm and judgement on others, and we remain curious about life itself. Being curious about our past, our present patterns and what threatens us as we consider change is key as we go forward from here.

Keep calm and keep journalling; it will all become clearer as we journey on.

Your Ripple

What comes to mind when you think of unpacking
your journey?

What kind of start in life did you have?

What threat, risk or challenge do you immediately think of
when you consider unpacking your journey?

What might stop you from being curious about yourself
and others?

What might keep you from journalling? What might help?

Chapter 2

Finding True Grit

To start unpacking the journey we need to see what we have inside. Have we got the grit to face it and keep going with it?

What lies before us in the unknown can be the scariest part. When we go through a big change, we can become full of fear of the unknown. During the writing of this book, two major life events have happened. First the United Kingdom left the European Union, an event that dominated the news and many people's thoughts for the best part of three years. I had friends who were stashing away teabags in case the world as we knew it, with all its comforts and essentials, might disappear overnight. Then coronavirus hit us! We were shut down almost overnight, and it wasn't just teabags that became scarce.

One of my worries – worse than that losing-the-cup-of-tea hit – was that hormone patches would be rationed following Brexit! Having been on HRT and enjoying feeling well again after a full hysterectomy following many years of illness, this could be a disaster! The threat of everything going backward health wise was a sudden realisation. No 'happy patch day' twice a week to keep me even and hormonally stable – that was a scary thought, not just for me but those around me!

Going back to the teabags, I certainly relate to this too. My morning cuppa is a real comfort for me, enabling me to start my day slowly, routinely climbing out of bed to make tea and then climbing back in again to ponder and plan my day.

Even just the thought that I might have to manage without either or both of these really is venturing into unknown territory! I am not sure I would like to be around me as I picture that scene! Just the threat of no patches creates an adverse reaction in me – the fear of the unknown, of losing control. I have gained true grit in my life to carry on in many difficult situations; could I find it within me to do it again without these things that keep me feeling safe and happy?

Yet all is actually calm at the moment, tea is flowing and patches are available for happy patch days. I stop and reflect on what is actually happening today. Nothing has happened; it is all simply a threat. I remind myself I have got through worse, so I would manage again if I needed to.

Most of us haven't been through a situation like the coronavirus before. So much more was at stake – much more than tea and hormone patches. Absolutely everything became uncertain and nothing could be taken for granted. It was a little like the situations people faced during the two World Wars, but this time with an invisible enemy.

A gritty person is one who sticks to their goals despite numerous issues, problems, setbacks and failures. The person has firmness of mind and unyielding courage. Synonyms of true grit are fortitude and determination. I have discovered this to be true in my own life, and somehow have managed to find true grit when it most mattered, and then realised that it had been there all along.

Deep in our psyche we may have fears that have their roots in a memory, a source of some kind of trauma to our very beings. It might be a sense of losing control, or a fear that something will take us down; it is anxiety that doesn't necessarily make sense in a given moment. We override this fear with an automatic defence mechanism that we do not even know is there any more. It's in our unconscious yet it plays out in our everyday. We defend our fears by changing our lifestyle, accommodating them daily.

Pressed But Not Crushed

After I had trained as a psychotherapist, I helped Malcolm Down with his new publishing company by going on an author visit. This was when I met the author who started the beginning of my own publishing career. This author is a man with true grit, and I will never forget his story. It was Andrew Davies, who wrote *Pressed But Not Crushed*.

Andrew had a stroke in his thirties which left him with locked-in syndrome, like Stephen Hawking. He went from being a young, married, fit and healthy man with a good career as a dentist, to being paralysed from the neck down.

When I read Andrew's book proposal before meeting him, I knew instantly that he was dyslexic. It was a mirror image of my essay reviews from university. Andrew had to overcome both his dyslexia and locked-in syndrome to get his book done. It took him two years. And Andrew continued to encourage me to work on my own book!

To meet Andrew was a daunting prospect, yet I left that meeting in total awe of him. After his prayers had been answered that he would be able to speak again, he would wait for his body to take a breath and then he would speak. He told us with such determination and even humour about his journey.

I felt that Emma, Andrew's wife, should write a chapter in the book. I knew we would need to treat her with kid gloves, so I offered to journey with her to help her to feel safe too. She explained that she had undiagnosed bipolar disorder when she married Andy, and he had stayed with her and took care of her. She was now doing the same for him.

What a privilege it was to sit with these two lovely people who had experienced such loss, pain and sadness, yet were still together on their journey. And this was the beginning of our journey with them.

We needed to make sure we protected them both; as Emma now cared for Andy she needed to stay well. She told us how miraculously she had been better since Andy's accident, and we needed to support her in every way we could.

The book came out quicker than we expected and even arrived on our desks a week earlier than we had anticipated. What a joy to see this being birthed!

Not only is this book a wonderful read, but despite his dyslexia Andy pressed in to organise an amazing black-tie book launch. He was one of the last to leave the dance floor in his wheelchair!

Having met Andy, I vowed that I would finish writing my own book because of his inspiration to finish the job. How could I not complete this task set before me?

It gives me great pleasure to see authors and clients in my private counselling practice, facing their deepest fears. Now that may sound odd, but the reason is that I can see them grow, and their lives change before my eyes. I have experienced a lot of pain, abuse and difficulties in my own life, and often wondered why this was my path. A special friend once said to me,

'You must be heading for something wonderful because you are going through so much.'

I felt like saying,

'It just can't be worth it, surely?!'

I went into my downstairs toilet and wiped away a tear of frustration. Then a starfish I had placed in there many years before struck a chord in my heart, and I was reminded again of the little boy throwing starfish back into the sea. I wanted to shout and scream,

'But what about me? Who will save me? This is too hard – I'm not sure I care for just one stranger right now!'

Yet in my heart I knew I would feel differently when this time had passed.

Well, now, thankfully, I can say that my struggles have helped more than just one person. Many people have come my way and I consider it a total privilege to help them along the way. The difference for me is that I am through the worst of my struggles, I hope!

I am now better at spotting my patterns. I have learnt when my line has been crossed and I speak out when it is too tough. This has come through my training, gaining self-awareness and being brave to act on it, most of the time! Just knowing this makes life more manageable. Struggles will inevitably come, and I know I have to stop and catch myself in order not to go down the road of the same thought processes I had developed to cope in my earlier life.

Learning to use that grit to survive this unpredictable and sometimes scary world can only really be mastered when we stop and listen to our internal voice, our frame of reference of how we see the world. By this I mean how we view ourselves and the world we are living in – our culture, our upbringing, our view of ourselves within it all. This usually happens when we hit a crisis and our coping mechanisms do not seem to work so well anymore.

As you are reading this, I hope that you will not wait for the crisis. Maybe you are in a strong place. So why not take some time to consider this before a crisis hits? This enables us to examine our emotions and our reactions to our circumstances, to make sense of them and reorder the way we look at them. This can be liberating – to realise that we have a choice.

Daring to be Vulnerable

Allowing ourselves to be vulnerable in front of another person is where more grit needs to be found, then the rewards follow. I believe that the safe space I create for clients is something I was seeking when I was younger. I grew up in a stepfamily of all boys, the youngest of six and the only girl, so my training in true grit started early.

We were fed on doorstop-sized sandwiches, beans on toast, or anything that would fill the boys up cheaply.

We were not permitted to speak during mealtimes, as we were to eat quickly and leave the table before my stepfather arrived home. The dogs would bark as a warning that his van had pulled up, and that signalled the end of the meal, no matter what was left on our plates. I know now that this was to allow my dad time and space on his return, but it was hard for me to chomp through a large sandwich of butter and jam at speed. It's not surprising that my relationship with food as I grew up was not an easy one.

Remembering good things that happened in my childhood has helped me keep a balanced view of the past. I have fond memories of holidays to Cornwall and Dorset, or the times when I dared to climb up lamp posts as my stepdad stood at the bottom, promising me 50p if I reached halfway. My brothers had to get to the top, and many times other kids from our street joined in. One of these kids, now in his fifties, has recently been in touch all the way from New Zealand, reminding me of what fun it was back then. Remember that lamp post!

Yet difficult and dark days seemed to dominate my memories for years. I struggled to even stay inside our home and would dread rainy days. I hated rain – I could smell it coming – as it meant being trapped inside. My needs were different from the boys', and my mum struggled to get this across to my stepdad. Many arguments took place, which led me to feel shame and guilt; consequently I was told to be less sensitive and to stop crying on many occasions, not to mention how many times I was hit and overruled by the boys. I learnt to suppress my emotions and cut off most of my feelings in order not to cry.

It was only when I became a Christian at the age of thirty that I learnt to be vulnerable again, and over time I even became thankful that I was sensitive. I found I had a sensitive spirit that could see things beyond the surface, start to heal and help others with their pain, if they were willing.

The Biggest Journey I Would Take

Here's how that happened – becoming a Christian, although for many years I thought you had to be born one or be baptised or invited in.

Little did I know that my life would change beyond recognition as I ventured into the biggest journey of my life. Having travelled and lived abroad, I thought my biggest journey had been done. In my early twenties I had adventured off on my own with a one-way ticket to New York. After two years of travelling all around the USA, Tahiti, Fiji, New Zealand, Australia and Thailand, I realised it was time to head home.

I missed my family, although I had met many interesting, dangerous and adventurous people along the way. Those stories will have to wait for now, as I would like to tell you about the next biggest journey I would take.

I had arrived home from my big trip around the world and met my handsome husband-to-be, Mark. We fell in love at first sight and got engaged after six weeks. We were married within a year, and launched straight into having our family. We had our lovely son Josh, and then Nicole followed quickly afterwards. When Nicole was six months old and still not sleeping and Josh a two-year-old boy bouncing around, all was not easy. It was wonderful, difficult and tiring all at once. Oh my, how I wanted to do it well!

I wanted to be a good mum and a good wife too, but nothing seemed to be going well. It became a competition between my husband and me as to who was more tired.

Where Is My Bed of Roses?

Having got married thinking that all my problems would be resolved, it was a shock to discover that we had marriage difficulties. Little did we know that our communication would be challenged by two young children and financial issues. Young, innocent and naive, but at least still in love – or so I thought, until I heard Mark say he was going to leave. I wanted to shout,

'But I'm saying I need more help!'

I sought help from my friend Karen, as she had mentioned that she knew of a good parenting course. I thought,

'That could help me, and maybe the rest will get easier.'

Karen told me there was a course starting the following week, led by her sister Janine. I went along, but as I was getting the children out of the car, a lovely lady called Bloss came out, saying,

'I'm so sorry, we're not running a parenting course. It's a marriage course, and I just wanted to let you know before you brought in the children.'

I looked up at the sky and thought,

'There is a God.' This was just what I needed, but I hadn't known such a thing existed! I had written a list the week before of what might help: Nicole to sleep, a playgroup for Josh, childcare for them both, help with my parenting skills, help with my marriage and something to help our communication, and perhaps a little break away together. It felt like the walls were coming in on me and I needed to get out of the house more. I happily went along and learnt to be loved by these ladies and watched my children settle in happily.

I was blown away by Janine, who was running a Care for the Family course written by Rob Parsons. Janine not only shared with us her own experience but was open to hear all our issues, her heart was so loving. She was registered blind yet still had the confidence to run this course for anyone who might walk through the door. This blew me away: her commitment to others, her loving nature and her love for Jesus just shone out of her.

This course provided so much support; I probably needed these wonderful people in my life more than I ever realised. All my needs were being met. Nicole started to sleep: I had told them how I was struggling, and then a book appeared, *How to Solve Your Child's Sleep Problems*. Josh had a wonderful time and used up a lot of energy so was happy to rest on his return home – phew! My husband and I went through the course together each week and our love blossomed again. It ended on our anniversary and we couldn't do or buy anything for each other that would match what we had just been given back. It was wonderful.

Then a friend rang me; I had told her we were having issues. She asked what she could do to help, and I said we needed a break. She sorted out for us to house-sit her brother's house in Somerset. This lovely retreat near Glastonbury became our holiday home for fifteen years. We also gained a lovely friendship with Jon and Caroline, leading to a wonderful godson, Cameron, and his sister Natalie becoming part of our lives.

Alpha Was the Beginning

I was encouraged to go on to do an Alpha course, which explained what Christianity was all about. On the third week I became fascinated that one of the leaders, Lesley, had a date in her Bible – it was the date when she had become a Christian. I was fascinated by that. She told me she had prayed a prayer which meant that from that day on she had a personal relationship with Jesus. I wanted to know how that happened and thought that I was at least a couple of years away from gaining understanding like that – I would have to study hard to find all the answers.

The next day, both my gorgeous children slept at the same time – I think these lovely ladies were praying, as that in itself was a miracle! I sat quietly, for fear of waking them, and read the little red booklet *Why Jesus?* It was all about to be in front of me rather than two years away . . .

Oh my gosh, those with a sensitive soul to spiritual things do look away now, as this will probably seem unbelievable. If it hadn't happened to me, I would struggle to believe it myself.

At the back of the *Why Jesus?* booklet was a prayer of forgiveness. I prayed it, even though I couldn't think of one thing I had done wrong. I laughed out loud, as I knew there *were* things, of course!

Next thing I saw my life rolling past my eyes, like an old cine film. Then there he was, right in front of me, standing before me: Jesus . . . yes, Jesus! The world stood still. He stood there, as alive as you or me. Such stature and strength. If only I could see that vision again today. I try to recreate it in my mind most days. I wept, and he put his hand on my head and blessed me. I didn't know much but I knew he was blessing me. I knew I was allowed to touch his robes, real and tangible. He was an almighty presence, perfect and strong. I said to him,

'You have always been there!'

It was as if a veil had been lifted; Jesus had been so close all the time, with just a thin veil between us, but I hadn't realised until now. I cried out to him and continued for hours at the relief of being able to finally let go. I felt like I had arrived home for the first time; nothing had ever felt that good before.

It took days to tell my husband what had happened. I kept trying, but it was so overwhelming I could not stop crying. To go from an outwardly calm, not very emotional young mum, to letting it all out at once was a bit of a shock to my husband. However, he finally got the full picture of what had happened, which was a great relief as I was concerned he might think I had lost my marbles! About three months later, as I shared my story in church, he made the same commitment, praying the prayer I had prayed.

Somehow, I had created an image in my mind of how Christians were: they were very good people. I was not particularly good and would not be able to keep that up even if I tried. I also thought they were all boring, so why would I join them? I really don't know why I had formed this opinion and feel a little embarrassed to share this rather ridiculous assumption with you.

However, other people's opinions of our new life values weren't always easy either, so once again my true grit defence for managing obstacles had to be used.

When we change or our lives change, this can be challenging to others. All we can do is own our part and keep being true to ourselves.

Mark and I journeyed together in our faith. When things began to go wrong eighteen years into our marriage, I stayed with my faith. His story is his story and I will leave it there. I have learnt that I am not responsible for his choices or path, even though I did give myself a hard time over this to begin with. We make choices along the way and have to stand by them. We can ask for forgiveness and turn our lives around, but it takes guts to swallow our pride.

I read a quote recently saying that no one died from choking on their pride. Probably one of the most attractive and appealing traits is when someone is vulnerable and asks for forgiveness. The opposite is also true, I believe: to try to look strong and stick to something out of stubbornness is not so pretty.

Forgiveness:

Take a look at the word forgiveness with me, for-give, give forward, the word 'for' bridges across time; past, present and future.

So if the word 'for' can be used when talking about the past, present or future. Bearing this in mind forgiveness is an act that can bridge all these time periods. An action to what has happened in the past, a decision given in the present and making a difference to the future. Powerful stuff!!

Letting go and forgiving someone is truly powerful. Forgiving ourselves and moving on is also very freeing. It cannot be over-egged or overrated – forgiveness is better for us all; our health, our relationships and our family will all benefit. We have no idea what other people are feeling and going through. It could be life-changing to contact someone and say you forgive them or to ask them for forgiveness. Being this vulnerable takes true grit.

Restoring the Fallen

Restoring the Fallen, a manuscript written by Mark and Cherith Stibbe, came to my attention. Mark had lived in secret and chaos. The need for truth and grace mixed into a situation, given some time, allows others to work things through and to begin to make sense where there is distress. As Mark found his way through this, lives began to be healed, which was helped by his honesty. He managed this by working with his therapist through the emotions that came up. He did not make light of this situation or just move away from his life, career and family, but instead chose to dig deep to find the root of his unhappiness.

First came *Home at Last*, his book on boarding school issues. I will cover more of this later in the chapter 'Boarded Heart' as I talk about the journey that has led others on through their pain of boarding school.

She Really Is Still Emily

Nothing is ever wasted, I have learnt, and I really enjoy hearing and reading about other people's experiences. Working with authors who have gone through so much, such as Emily Owen as we worked on her book *Still Emily*, remind me of how critical it is to keep going, to keep pressing through the tough times and then to re-evaluate.

Emily's life would never be the same after surgery left her deaf. Mine would not be the same after my marriage ended after twenty years. Both of us would have needed to be honest and to want to work at the marriage to keep it going.

Distractions would have needed to be talked about and decisions made together. I did not get this opportunity, so I had to work with being a single parent going forward. However, it was essential for me to take what was left of the situation and make the most of it.

Among many issues resulting from a devastating degenerative illness, Emily lost her hearing, yet she writes with such flair and clarity. Working with Emily and learning to see how she operated taught me so much.

I would try to encourage her to bring more emotion out of her story, and she would say an emphatic 'No!' and we left those areas alone. I do remember a time when, after about three days she came back and said, 'OK, I get what you mean here; I trust you. Let's go with it.' As long as she was well and feeling safe, we carried on.

Emily has remained open and teachable and has not given in to the isolation that can come with deafness, let alone the anxiety and fear of what's ahead. I was so proud to see her on TBN television's *Facing the Canon* with J.John as he interviewed her about her illness and faith. How scary, yet she says 'yes' to every opportunity, as she knows it may help others. Emily approaches these opportunities with such a humble spirit and with such gratitude to others and for her life. She is a pleasure to work with and someone I am thankful I can call a friend.

Emily's book is available in audio form to help those who are visually impaired to enjoy her book. We are all thrilled with that, as we are reaching more and more people with disabilities. We try where we can, as a publishing house, to think out of the box and reach anyone our books might help. We are all thankful to Torch Trust for the Blind for helping those with sight issues and putting our books into accessible forms for those with sight loss and impairment.

No Soft Landing

My children were my blessing from my marriage, and they became my reason to keep going when it fell apart. They were my purpose in the times that could have taken me down. There were many moments of despair that I felt would engulf me, but I had to find the strength deep within to model to them how to keep going.

I thank God for my two wonderful, now grown-up children. I wish their experience of life could have been as perfect and protected as I had planned. However, I realised I could not cushion their lives forever, and these times will have helped them to grow strong with true grit to press on at times in the future that are difficult. I know they both have it in them to manage this and also to help others.

Stepping Into the Gap

Stepping into the gap to help others: a good example of this is my lovely caring son Josh while he was at Royal Holloway University enjoying his studies and sports. Sadly, one day he rang me to say that a friend and member of his Ultimate Frisbee team had passed away.

He had not turned up for practice and they had begun to worry about him. They were then told that he had been hit by a train earlier that morning. Later, Josh discovered Cameron had committed suicide, which was so tragic. The team have since raised money for the charity that was set up by Cameron's parents for mental health awareness.

Josh was captain of the team, so he stepped out to start a Facebook group to support the team. He made himself available to others to help. My heart ached for him, yet I was so proud of him as he handled it so well. It did affect him, as he was deeply saddened and shocked. He may have been helping others to ease his own pain. I also believe he used his difficult experience of the loss of relationship with his father to help others. True grit deep within: we don't know how we will handle things in a crisis, but experience tells me that Josh will be OK as long as he gives himself time to grieve.

Finding determination to press on despite circumstances is something we have all had to learn to do recently. Finding that true grit deep within is really not something we go looking for, but we tend to find it accidentally when the going gets tough.

Taking Off the Mask

Another gritty person I have had the pleasure of meeting is Claire Musters and of reading her book *Taking Off the Mask*. To encourage us to take our masks off, to freely be who God created us to be, Claire had to take hers off and tell us her story. Moving away from disappointment and shame to be who we fully can be in God, Claire has made herself vulnerable within the Christian arena to allow others to do the same.

True grit seemed so relevant when I reflected on the story of one particular client as we ventured together in equine therapy.

John Wayne came to mind only after I realised where I had heard the term 'true grit' before.[1] Growing up with so many brothers, I had little say in what I watched, and it is only now I see the influence. I watched many films and played many fighting games in this male world. I learnt many rugby songs too, which I am not sure helped to equip me for life! Yet the fight I needed to survive at times may well have been enhanced by this early outlook.

Not So Nice to Rice

One funny story my children loved was when I met former Arsenal footballer Pat Rice at a health club we both attended. I was told he was around, yet I didn't know who he was and was not aware he was about to walk in. He walked up to me and shook my hand, saying,

'Are you into football?'

My reply just slipped out:

'Not really. I grew up on the side of a rugby pitch. Although when I was a teenager I did support Spurs.'

On hearing that he spun on his heels and walked out. Thankfully, with his dry sense of humour, he returned to name me

'the lovely lady from the dark side'.

I think my straight-talking at times could have got me into some trouble, but it's not with intent to harm!

---

[1] *True Grit* was the name of a 1969 film starring John Wayne. It was remade in 2010 with Jeff Bridges, Matt Damon and Josh Brolin.

I recognise it as part of my survival coping mechanism stemming from the fear of being teased and put down by a man, so I would sometimes get in there first. Pat was probably just being friendly, and I jumped the gun. However, he did get me back many times as we shared cups of tea together in our health club, accompanied by much banter and teasing.

The way we are brought up can stay with us, even though we want to step away from it. Being teased a lot during my childhood, I learnt to defend by teasing.

As I reflect on this relationship with Pat, it was fun, but if I was feeling vulnerable, I would need to avoid the teasing even though it was all in good humour. I am learning, as we all can, to deal with vulnerability better, having read Brené Brown's *Daring Greatly*. Brené has spent many years studying shame. You can hear her on YouTube and TED Talks. I will cover more a little later on, but, in brief, she talks of shame shields that we hide behind and defend ourselves with. They represent moving away, moving forward and moving against the sense of attack on us. They work as a defence for immediate survival, but over time need to be addressed. Shame cannot survive when spoken out, as our triggers of shame become known to us and we stop operating from them.

Right Advice at the Right Time

The fight to survive in the male-dominated home I believe became part of my being. Since then, I have had to learn to know when not to fight, to just be, to let things ripple out and to be me, and not to try so hard: less striving and more living. I'm still learning, while also feeling thankful that I have this stamina.

I was thankful that my GP, Dr Turner, advised me that my counselling course would see me through my marriage breakup. I thank him from the bottom of my heart for not giving up on me. I asked for sleeping tablets and antidepressants to get me through but he refused, saying, 'You are going to need your wits about you and your counselling course will be your way through.'

I saw Dr Turner many times as he checked up on me, asking me how it was going and how my children were. I am so grateful for his approach of listening and being there for me.

Along with this, having gained true grit from my background has given me the strength to push on when times are tough, and to be there for others.

I want to help others find a good way through that will not trip them up at a later date. I have wanted so much to help others find a way of talking out their issues, of going with and admitting it is a bad day or period of time. To be able to stay with this and not want to drown it out or suppress it but to feel the emotions is important to make progress.

Something that stood out to me with a broken marriage behind me was that I felt labelled by being 'divorced' – how I hated that box being ticked. This had happened to me; now my life was changed forever and I was holding the shame of a 'failed marriage'. That was never my plan – the complete opposite was true, and we had even run marriage courses to stop this happening to others.

Then I read that failure isn't being knocked down; rather, it's not getting back up again.

That tapped into my very core and I knew this was it – I had to get back up, whatever that looked like.

Who am I now?

What was I getting back up for?

I was no longer Mark's wife, but a single person.

Again, digging deep and finding strength that I didn't know I had to turn things around, how would that help others?

Desperate Measures

The strength I found gave me the passion to try anything to help other people find their way through. An example of this was a client I saw after she had been diagnosed with dyslexia while taking her mock GCSEs.

She had been struggling in many ways, which had led to eating issues. This was becoming urgent and I was praying for a way through. I was considering equine therapy. She arrived for her session but was unable to get out of the car, so I put it to her mum:
   'I was wondering if Beth is interested in horses?'
'Well, we've just booked a holiday in Canada on a ranch.'
   That was the confirmation we all needed, so equine therapy started.

It takes courage to step out, and it had been years since I had been involved with horses, and I wasn't missing it. To be honest with you, I was still afraid of them. I had been keen on all animals while I was growing up. When I was young, I really wanted a Shetland pony (made for people of my height, I thought!). Having studied Agricultural Administration at college, I had been around horses and had ridden on and off, but never really felt totally confident.

Having been thrown a few times I was a little fearful around horses, so equine therapy was a major move forward for me too. A lot of trust has been exercised through these relationships and we have all benefited, and I definitely believe that Turko, the horse, enjoys all the attention. I am so thankful, too, for this wonderful lady who has happily shared her gorgeous horses with us.

I was working with dogs in therapy and I felt that horses would be another creative way of connecting with this client. Sometimes it has just been right to start running with what feels set before me. Thankfully, so far my instincts have been right, and I have seen some amazing turnarounds. While the horses were being managed by someone else, I could talk with Beth. It really helped to be out in the fresh air, walking together rather than sitting face to face, which I believe had felt a bit threatening for her. The whole environment worked for Beth. She relaxed and connected with the horses instantly.

The therapy was relaxed and light as we made connections with emotions, with the horse and with each other as we shared the experience. We related issues such as controlling the horse to controlling her feelings: it takes time and patience. Beth made a wonderful connection with Turko, the freckly boy. I have seen many times that this can be a double-edged sword: I also connected with Turko and missed him when we had a break.

It was a wonderful distraction, away from stress, up on a beautiful hill surrounded by a circle of high trees in the distance. The English countryside at its best provided the backdrop for a healing heart as Beth's emotions began to calm and make sense.

The aim was to help her learn to control her emotions again rather than allowing them to run away with her, to enable her to calm her mind and help her to listen to her body. Controlling Turko when he seemed to want to race away may have caused anxiety, but as I talked with her, we discussed how this felt so similar.

Beth was more aware of her body while riding. This is a good way to be in the moment – bodily and emotionally aware. Molly, the other horse, started to feel left out. She would watch as Turko was given so much attention. One week she decided to be brave and joined in with the grooming. Beth even got a hug from her, totally unexpectedly! We have all grown through the therapy!

Many conversations unfolded as Beth's confidence improved. It was a total pleasure to see the huge smile appear on her face. I knew in my heart that she would be helping other young girls through similar pain as she came through it. Then in one session she told me she was helping a twelve-year-old who was self-harming and experiencing emotional distress. My heart leapt as I heard this, and I encouraged Beth to see how far she had come and that she was never alone, even though at times it might feel like it. I reminded her to not hold this too heavily on her shoulders and to reach out to share with other adults and professionals. She saw how blessed she was to have parents who loved her so much and were able to show it, and she began to see the privileges in her life. Her faith grew again in herself, in her family, in her church and in God.

What a wonderful turnaround. I am privileged to have been a part of this story.

Life Is a Risk

A book on growing and transformation would not be complete without a further mention of Brené Brown. In *Daring Greatly* she speaks of how the courage to be vulnerable transforms the way we live, love, parent and lead. Wow! Allowing the walls to come down can lead to such a fulfilled life! I felt vulnerable even picking up her book, so now why write my own? She's done it, and I could just refer clients to hers. Yet, no . . . I have my story to tell, a story that will magnify and enhance the ripple that Brené has brought to our attention.

Those who have made my acquaintance will no doubt know I like warmth and water, so if I am at home in the UK where there isn't always much sun, I like to be by a pool or in a sauna as often as I can. This helps me unwind and regenerate as I am aware of my need to take care of my own emotional and physical state. I will explore later why water and warmth do this for me.

My friends know that I often get into conversations that may appear random or deep quite quickly. My children have stopped asking me now,
'how on earth did you find that out from someone you have never met before?' or,
'I didn't know you knew that person.'

Often this is with complete strangers, but by grace I seem to be able to make connections where I least expect them. Maybe it's by not expecting them that the door is open and I just let it happen, I'm not entirely sure!

Here is an example of finding out something I would never have experienced about life and death within a hospital setting. Stephen, a hospital manager, shared with me that the most death and compensation cases come from the maternity wing. That was a reality check, as I have such fond memories of leaving with my new little pink or blue bundle to love. Yet it struck a chord with me: that's the beginning, and if it starts perilously, how do we process this without a memory?

The beginning of life means leaving the known, the womb, and venturing into the unknown via a dark and almost impossible route. We leave the comfort of the warm waters – perhaps this is why many of us like water around us to help us relax. Others enjoy skydiving, the feeling of being weightless again. Under stress, many return to sucking their thumb and curling up: 'I'm just looking forward to curling up on the sofa.'

Comfort, rest, warmth, safety: something known.

We don't know that it will all change one day. Is this our unconscious mind trying to get us back to safety, the warmth of the bubble around us?

I wonder if this is why water and saunas make me happy, relaxed and calm: perhaps it stimulates memory of the womb. This safety and comfort cannot be spoken, as it actually goes deeper than we can put into words. This led me to wonder whether we long to get back to that. Am I missing this deep-beyond-words connection with another – in this case my mother?

Watching a mother breastfeeding a child can be the sweetest thing, yet in our society we have made it secretive and unpleasant. This made me question, are we wanting to gain that connection back? Is this interpreted as a sexual urge which can be seen as bad too? Yet we are all here now, and millions before us, through the intimate connection of two people. It's more acceptable to talk about intimacy and lovemaking these days, but we still squirm just slightly, if we are honest.

I have pondered this word many times – intimacy – I have played with it, feared it and dismantled it.

In-ti-ma-cy – in to me you see. We seek this, yet it scares us too.

To be totally seen is the full connection we crave, yet being totally seen is also a place of vulnerability.

When we take this to a close, personal level, physically connecting, we may have thoughts such as, that's bad, private, not to be discussed, naughty, unacceptable or even dirty.

Stop for a moment and think about what comes to mind for you. What are the negatives? What are the immediate thoughts that you may want to brush away? Stay with those, as they are probably the most telling of your experiences or perceptions of having been or of being intimate with someone.
One book I was involved in publishing contained an intimate scene between a husband and wife. This book was banned from one bookshop in the USA because of this section.

Was *The Fate of Kings*,[2] by Mark Stibbe, too real for some of our fellow Christians? We sold more in the UK as people were trying to find it and form an opinion about it, so its fate wasn't all bad. But we have to be real – that physical intimacy needs to happen to make babies, and it will keep happening, otherwise we will die out as a race. We are hardwired for intimacy and connection – even Christians!

I recently saw on social media, a post that said, 'Young people of today don't want children, so we have a major problem as the human race may fade out.' I feel this is more of a concern than knowing a married couple have an intimate relationship. As a therapist, it would concern me if a married couple didn't touch each other and enjoy each other, yet with my publishing hat on I would wonder how you are feeling reading about this. However, I will carry on, as such intimacy leads to being created in a loving relationship and arriving in a loving environment.

This is obviously the ideal, yet there is no perfect parent, no matter how hard we try. So we, as the children of these parents, will all have issues to unpack. Just like Paul in the Bible, we all have a thorn in the side (2 Corinthians 12:7), but we don't need to leave it there. Let's get real and unpack our issues around feeling and connecting and hide less behind fear.

It is worth exploring whether there is an innate longing to get back to safety and whether, for men, women hold that key.
 'You have the womb, the location of my peace and safety.'

---

[2] Mark Stibbe and G.P. Taylor, *The Fate of Kings* (Malcolm Down Publishing, 2017).

Then what is it for a woman to hold that ability to create a new life within a safe space, and also to be held safely by a man?

Yet life starts with love, being loved and being held safe in love, unconditional love we all crave.

Going Back to Go Forward

So, going back to the beginning, all our lives start with a perilous journey. We survive that, then there is more unknown as we cry for food: will it come? There are uncomfortable feelings of cold, heat, wetness, soreness or pain. How do we ask for what we want? We cry out.

I have seen a baby cry until she was beyond herself. The sadness of that face has stayed with me as if I saw it yesterday. She was all cried out. At that point something breaks inside, and it can then take a lifetime to try to resolve that pain, hurt and damage. We can travel through life's journey unknowingly trying to resolve this unacknowledged pain to reach a level of acceptance within ourselves. Maybe full healing can come, along with a sense of feeling whole again. This is a tough journey to go on, facing the inner fear of what we might find:

- ► Will I find nothing at all?
- ► Will I like what I find?
- ► What am I here for?
- ► What's it all about?

Gracelets

Intimacy – life is a risk – we have to allow ourselves to be vulnerable to grow in intimacy, to allow ourselves to see what is going on underneath the smile. Allowing others in is another level: 'in to me you see'. Will you like it? Can I bear it?

The fear of what we may find is far more powerful than reality. You are uniquely and wonderfully made, so you may be pleasantly surprised.

Many of the stories in this chapter of people with faith speak for themselves. I hope you find them encouraging to take a step further in your spiritual journey or to start to awaken your spirit. You have one, you are a whole person, so let us see what happens when you take that step too.

Jesus demonstrated a new way to be, to forgive and to love in fullness. It doesn't mean we forget and become doormats, but it does stop us stewing in our own juices. This is what can make us physically ill, so it's of benefit to us and to others around us.

We can remain with the pain of the past, as it is what we know. This may sound extreme, but we can actually sit contentedly with that rather than push on to the final place of contentment. Known may be painful, but it feels safe. Finding true grit to move from this place means you will not need to look back any more.

Your Ripple

You may be wondering how you have managed through some of those times. I also hope you found it a time of growth, beyond just survival.

Taking this from another angle, what happens when it's your doing that things have become broken and need replacing?

Can you find the true grit to explore a way of repairing what is broken and replace the outdated?

Can you find a heroic path of telling the truth and move on?
   It is extremely hard sometimes to find the strength to take the responsibility of our individual place in the world, our very being.

It takes true grit to forgive. Who in your life would benefit from your forgiveness?

Can you see your life being better for having forgiven them?

What might be painful, a familiar, known pain that is hard to get past?

The questions below may help with this:

- ▶ If I let this go, what will I find?
- ▶ Will I find nothing at all?
- ▶ Will I like what I find?

Chapter 3

A Friend or a Fraud

Through this chapter we will explore how we have managed to delude ourselves to avoid seeing our fears and anxieties. They blind us in order to protect us. Fear is inbuilt to protect us, but it can get out of hand, overworking without us knowing. Usually it is because something has happened to us, or we have taken in a belief, and we have then overridden it to survive or spare us from pain.

A simple example of this is the fear of heights. This fear can be a really good thing to stop us walking off the edge of a cliff. But when the fear gets out of hand and we can no longer get into a lift, which is safe and reliable (unless this has been proven otherwise), then we know this fear is no longer helping us. This is a very simplified example, but I hope it gives you an idea of how coping mechanisms can start to rule our lives and take away our freedom.

Fears Handed Down to Us

Most of our issues come from when were young, so they are pushed deep into our psyche. We have tried to bury pain from the past so we may not know exactly what it is. There are no perfect parents, as we have said, and we live in a fallen world, so our upbringing would have inevitably contained moments when we were failed or let down. This is especially the case from the time when the advice given was to let babies cry. There may be wounds that have come from previous generations. The past has sent out a ripple, creating a way of being from our predecessors. This has brought us to where we are today; geographically, in our way of being and in how we see the world. Some of this will be known to us and some isn't; some of it is good and some is bad.

We only need to look at the Jewish history to see how its strong roots affect this and previous generations. People still visit Poland and Berlin to experience the enormity of the devastation of the concentration camps. This gives us some understanding of what that generation went through. It is there strongly in the ripple, and it will be sensed down the generations even without a conversation needing to take place.

 It may be an underlying sense, a sadness, a strength; however it is described, it is there. It needs to be seen, understood and accepted in order that the healing and power of this can be used going forward. Like for all of us, making peace with our past in our own way is how we can go forward fully living. For most of us it is more deeply hidden than it is in the Jewish community, so it takes time to stop and look.

We Can't Go Around It . . .

The past brings us to the here and now, when we need to go to the heartache. Where there has been pain in our lives, we need to look at the heartbreak. Unfortunately there is no way around it, as whatever we push down, knowingly or unknowingly, stays there until we are brave enough to confront it. It does not go away.

If we ignore it and hope it goes away, brushing it under the carpet, we will eventually fall over the little mountain of debris.

Sadly, this quite often comes out in health issues, whether mental health, emotional distress, an anxious spirit or physical sickness. It has to find its way out, and wherever your weakness is it will likely pop out when you are least expecting it. Yet we push it all down, thinking we are keeping control, but this is part of the illusion: keep everything hidden so that you are in control. No one will know. Yet we all know someone who is stressed and is a bit shocked when we mention it to them, as they think they're doing a good job of covering it up.

I hope this is your time to take a look and see what might have been buried in your life. Stay with me and see why this chapter is called 'A Friend or a Fraud'. This friend is someone who has protected you, shielded you and helped you along the way. This friend has been there probably for a very long time, maybe even since you were a young child. The 'true you' may actually never have been seen, because the friend has been someone to hide behind. I have both experienced this myself and worked with many clients, especially those who went to boarding school – hence a boarded heart to preserve the self, the true you.

A false self has to be created to survive, and this is the new friend. It is a new way of being around people, yet we know deep inside that this is not really who we are. We hear ourselves saying things and see ourselves doing things, yet we wonder why we say and do them. Unfortunately, we convince ourselves that this is who we are, reinforcing the message of who we have been told we are. This could be from parents, friends, teachers and the media.

This is a chance to find that real person, to discover who you were created to be. This is when a sense of freedom and empowerment starts to offer a glimmer of hope, even elation. It is the most exciting journey we can go on, truly knowing and finding ourselves. You can find yourselves in the midst of a crisis; even if life is good, there is always something we can learn and grow from.

Reflecting Ripple of Pain

Let me share the story of a young girl who was sent away to boarding school. She is one of four Jewish daughters and the only one who was sent. She doesn't know why, but she believes it must have been because she was different, difficult or that something was wrong with her.

The matron took a disliking to her and bullied her. When she went home, she couldn't share because she was already 'a problem'. She didn't fit in at home any more as it was unfamiliar, yet she was dreadfully unhappy at the institution, now her home.

Boarding school does not tend to celebrate femininity, so this too can get lost along the way. Years down the line this woman has not really found her own way of being. She has also turned away from her faith and feels that she just does not fit in anywhere.

In adulthood she met a lady who was feminine, had a strong faith and was following her dreams. She was the opposite of her, yet she reminded her of her past. She had lost both these elements of her life.

She was reminded of being different, and consequently she found it difficult to manage her reaction to this lady.

Eventually, through therapy, she was able to see how she has become aggressive towards this lady as a result of frustration at her own past. The therapy eventually enabled her to find acceptance of the pain and anger. She was then able to approach the lady to ask to be forgiven for her attitude.

The response she received was,
'I wondered what I had done to you, but finally I see it was not me at all. I was a mirror showing you your pain. I used to feel angry with you but now I feel sorry that you had to go through that and that I had to go there with you.'

Peace was made between them and they moved on. There was no longer a sense of needing to resolve something; it was understood.

Invisible Barbed Wire

If we do not face these issues, we carry them. You yourself may have been on the receiving end of the pain others are carrying. In some relationships it can feel as though it leaks out. This is known as passive anger, a sudden remark or action that catches you out. I have known this to be so strong it feels like a snake that suddenly bites me from behind just as I relax.

In situations where there is offence that has not been explored, this can be difficult. I knew of a situation where one lady would walk out of the room every time another lady walked in. No one else noticed, and the first lady had to bear this constant rejection every time they were at a social gathering.

Highlighting issues such as this to others can help gain support, and others may notice, like something hidden behind a blind spot coming into view. The behaviour is then seen and can be explored. It is not always as painful as this rejection, but it will likely have a root of pain or fear of pain.

Our false self, our 'friend' who is there to protect us, fraudulent yet effective, will convince us that it is safer and better to leave these issues alone. They will cause pain and should be buried. Yet causing pain is exactly what they are still doing in our everyday lives. They may seem like the kindest and gentlest of people, yet comments they make seem to stick in your mind. Barbed comments, even when they are delivered with a laugh or in a childish manner, still hurt and stick.

Take a moment . . .

- ▶ Do you ever do this to yourself: everything is going well but a negative thought pops up, leaking in to steal the moment?
- ▶ Whose voice is it? Can you stay with it and see where it is coming from?

Our parents and siblings are a big influence if we have the privilege of growing up in our own childhood home. The influence will be strong, and often this is a voice from those years. Let's stay with that and see how it is leading you each day.

Can you speak out about your feelings of anger and frustration, or do you find yourself delivering a subtle comment when stressed or under pressure?

Exposing the Friend

Truly knowing and understanding ourselves and being in touch with our deepest feelings is what can bring contentment. A line in the sand, no going back and repeating the upheaval of the emotions that link to an event. However, first we need to truly go there, to find out what is behind the acting out that happens when we are stressed or anxious.

These protective strategies can leave us feeling like a fraud – once we know about it is happening, it can leave us wondering if it is a friend or a fraud. As we let this friend stay with us and collaborate with it, even if we are not aware of it, we collude with it. Wouldn't it be great to check out this friend we have created, to accept that it has worked to bring us this far but now it is time to take a closer look?

Maybe 'fraud' describes how you feel, or maybe it's more of a sense of loss or disappointment that lingers. Many people experience what they term as 'depression' – dark days that are hard to pull themselves out of. This sense of anguish is understandable as feelings are pushed, pressed down – depressed, leading to depression. It's in the very word: depressed.

How can we release these feelings and start living a more 'impressive' life with real friends? It's not OK to be half living, feeling like a fraud and not really managing as well as the impression we give. How about allowing your true, more impressive self to become real?

To start this process, we can take a positive moment, when we are in a good place and can catch a moment in time when we can say,

'This is good. I feel happy and comfortable in myself right now.'

Catch that moment. Hold it like a freeze-frame picture – shut your eyes and stay with it. We can do that now by recreating that good feeling in our mind. Many a sunset has led me to one of those 'life is good' moments.

- ► What is it that is good?
- ► Is it the external or is it something deeper inside that is calm and content?

It can be hard to stay with this good feeling; we may find our defences are there in a heartbeat. Straight away, our fear of losing the good can jump out of nowhere and steal the moment. Now which is the false self – your 'friend' – and which is the true self?

So let's get back to the unpacking. That nagging voice in our heads and the anxiety held in our bodies are evidence that there is something that needs attention. I have found when I am struggling to not stay in the moment I jump ahead to, 'it will be all right when . . .'

Let's break down those thoughts and feelings that come from our heart and head.

Remember as we go through this that we will be pursuing that 'peaceful contented feeling' as it glimmers through at any stage of our journey. It's not just about arriving somewhere, but it's also about enjoying the good bits along the journey.

Once we have seen and felt the fullness, moments of contentment within when we are no longer the fraud but truly ourselves, we can find and observe our emotional patterns and general state of health more readily. I tell clients regularly that it is like going to the gym – the more we go, the more routine it becomes without so much effort. But, in the beginning, it has to be a choice to push against the mind and body.

Our emotional state affects everything. It affects our everyday and everybody around us, so it's worth doing this for them even if you can't do it for yourself. However, I would prefer you did it for you, as you are more likely to go the full distance.

Coming Out Gold

As I was writing this chapter, a client came into my counselling room having been away for a long break. It has always been enlightening and engaging working with her, but this session was rather special. She presented information about four generations of males in her family who were all cut off emotionally, empty and distant. We looked back at her great-grandfather, who had abandoned his wife and children. I wondered what had happened to him, as maybe it went even further back. In such situations, I will often think or ask,
'What happened to them?' rather than,
'What is wrong with them?'

We talked about the ripple effect of each generation and how this had played out. One sad effect of this was that pornography had come down the line. I had been aware of this from previous sessions so I had recommended *Coming Out Gold* by Rob Joy.

In Rob's book he shares his story and offers sound advice for men and their families on how to move away and move on from pornography. This book had helped her enormously, especially as she read Rob's wife's chapter. My client felt she had managed to forgive those in her life, but she felt emotional about it again.

'Why can I not just forgive and move on? Why does it still hurt?'

'There are many layers to a deep hurt such as this,' I replied, '
which we can continue to discover even though we have forgiven.' Tears began to fall.

'I feel disappointed and hurt. Was I not enough?'

'Looking at the pattern within the male line, it would seem that you and your husband were drawn together because you are a strong person who showed him respect. However, you could not make him whole – this was his responsibility to work through. If he was unable to speak out his frustrations and anger, these emotions may have become confused within him so that he acted it out sexually. Sexual drive can be very strong. This could have been a way of taking the power back from you and from women generally. Deep anger with his mum was likely the root of his pain. This appears to have been an issue throughout the male line, this way of releasing pain and gaining back control.

This is not a reflection on you, but sadly you were caught up in it. It is complex when things go wrong, especially when we are young. Maybe he never was given the opportunity to face his issues, or he chose not to. Fear of bringing this into the light seemed too much for him.'

Making sense of this, not excuses, helped this lady to see that it was his 'stuff' rather than hers. Left unresolved, this could cause damage to her own self-esteem; she would be tempted to blame herself, causing deep shame and creating an issue with her body image – a further negative ripple going out and causing more suffering. Yet speaking this out helped her to make sense of it and gave her peace.

'So it wasn't me, my body, whether or not I lost weight or the fact that I didn't understand what was going on in his mind?'

'If he didn't share, you were unlikely to be able to know what was going on for him. I know this has hurt you deeply. Pornography takes away dignity and undervalues a woman's femininity and sexuality. I do hear the pain you are going through.'

After a pause, to allow tears, I asked,
'Did you have times of intimacy?'

'Yes, we did. They were very special.'

'You felt he was present and engaging with you?'

'Yes, he was.'

'Please hold on to that. This is not anything about your appearance or you as a wife; it was a way of managing his emotions, an unhealthy way to escape from difficult feelings which would have left him feeling even more empty and isolated.'

'He would have been struggling alone,' she said.

'Sadly, yes. This would have been an inward struggle for him that he believed he was protecting you from, yet it did not work. I'm sorry you have had to suffer this and to experience the deceit. If he would have spoken out about his pain, let his guard down, he would have had time to resolve this within himself and give you the space to resolve it with him.'

Sadly, her husband had passed away, so she was left with unanswered questions.

As we can see from this client exchange, the husband had created a fraud to present as though nothing was wrong, yet it was harming him, his wife and his children. As this is now being addressed in the family, the ripple of pain resulting from pornography hopefully will stop at this generation as it is being brought into the light.

Exposing pain is hard. It makes us feel vulnerable, almost naked. The thought of sharing with someone outside the family, such as a counsellor, can feel terrifying, but for many, when it comes out it is a relief. This is far better than going through life feeling like an imposter, which sadly this man probably felt in his own marriage because he was hiding a dark secret.

It takes bravery to step out and break these patterns of behaviour, and this client is staying there for her own resolution within herself and for her children.

Imposter Within

This sense of feeling like a fraud is also known as imposter syndrome. Sometimes it is real – faking it really does happen – yet most of the time it is a way of managing fear. This man would have feared his whole world falling apart if it was known he was relying on pornography. He would have feared devastating his family, their reputation and everything collapsing around him. What a tremendous weight to carry.

The past does influence our present and our future, but if we stop and take a look at the effects, we can then change our way of being in the future. We can change the narrative by listening to the thoughts we have and being aware of them, and as we begin to understand them, we gain power over them.

A False World

While counselling I see young people suffering from OCD (obsessive compulsive disorder) and anxiety from as young as eight years old. I have found that the more we speak openly and give young people the truth, the less they are likely to be anxious. Often it is the creation of an unknown and false world, an illusion that we have produced to protect them, that actually has the opposite effect. It is then a shock when something happens as they have no way of processing it. We need to give them the tools to cope with life challenges but, like the air steward would say, we need to put our own oxygen mask on first, and then help others.

Let's look at our own patterns, especially us parents, so that we are better equipped to be honest and to help our young people. If we do not help them, they will search for their own way through, which may not be helpful at all in the long term.

They may find their own tools and crutches, such as pornography, drugs and drink. When they can't cope, they wonder what is wrong with them, especially if there is conflict with parents. Self-harm is on the rise partly because of this dilemma. It's a way of taking back control and preserving those around them – again, sadly, a complexity of our fallen world. So it's best we explore the challenges in life with our children when they are young and learn the lessons with them along the way. Talking, listening, more talking and listening: I cannot encourage communication enough, even when they are pushing you away.

Finding Yourself While Being Mum

One of the hardest roles in life is being a parent, yet it is the most rewarding of all when it is going well and there are times to celebrate. Like giving birth, the pain is forgotten when we see the reward. When women go back to work after bringing up a family, or while their children are still young, this can be another time of feeling a fraud.

I would like to encourage working mums to find themselves again in their new roles in life. We may feel as though we are faking it as we strive to make our home and work life good for everyone around us. We may believe we are not giving enough time to our children or to our job and feel split between the two. Along the way it is easy to forget that our own dreams and desires are still significant and need to be listened to.

It seems difficult to be on top of our game – we might believe our skills are lacking, particularly if we have stayed at home with children for a number of years. But we need to recognise the skills we have gained in managing the home and children while our partners have continued their careers.

Perhaps if we valued this more, the world would too. This could be an ideal we are aiming at but so worth considering, so that we can change patterns that seem to keep occurring in society.

Classic Example

One client shared with me,
'I am not like other women in the business. I don't wear jewellery and glamorous clothes. I worry he will lose interest in me. I like being at home and he will be travelling and meeting new people.'

It is crucial to value the asset of 'being there' and being the best we can be, enjoying the home and the children, and making it the best it can be while he is away. Celebrating him when he comes home should be enough, as long as there are no significant underlying issues within the marriage. This is another clear example of how we need to face that fraudulent feeling when it arises and recognise that what we have before us has great worth.

Women who are working and travelling may feel guilty for leaving their children, and they need to know they are still doing a good job. They are still Mum, giving to their children, not just financially, and they are also able to give to society in the business world.

Yet that voice can creep in, saying things like:

- ▶ 'You are not a good enough mum.'
- ▶ 'Women are not as important or valued as much as men in the workplace.'
- ▶ 'You are not doing either role well.'
- ▶ 'You are failing at both.'
- ▶

Let these anxieties out and acknowledge the voice as an imposter. Often this is a voice from the past:

- ▶ 'You will never make it.'
- ▶ 'You will never measure up.'
- ▶ 'You could do better.'

Such voices and thoughts are often the driving force to perform and succeed, but what does that actually look like in the day-to-day? Those who choose to unpack the anxiety and make themselves vulnerable to voice these thoughts are often surprised to realise where they come from. Many driven people are hiding a vulnerable area of themselves; arrogant behaviour can often be a form of hiding this. I believe the bigger the wall, the bigger the vulnerability. We will talk more about this in the chapter 'Feeling Not Filling'.

Top of the Tree: Scary Place to Be

I have journeyed with many who have reached great heights and there seems to be a familiar theme; one such person said,
'This probably won't make sense, but I have to say it . . . I feel like a fraud. I've blagged my way to the top and I don't know how I've done it, because I can't do it.'

Living with my 'secret weapon' of dyslexia (which I will unpack more later), I know the feeling of trying so hard to remain confident. I am thankful that I can understand others with this same sense of,
'Any moment now they'll figure out I can't do this and it will all end.

'It is a deep fear and a deep hope all in one. It will be over. This hard work of life and doing what I am doing will come to an end. Yet the fear stays dormant until it is spoken about.'

'So how long did you do this work for?'

'Twenty years, and I retired recently. What a relief!'

'Do you still feel like a fraud when you look back and see what you have achieved?'

'Absolutely!'

'OK, let's look at your achievements . . . Wow, you did all of that, and you rose to the top of the company, and now they want you to mentor others because of who you are?'

'Yes.'

We look together at these achievements and, as we do, a smile breaks out. He sees he could do it, did do it and is still doing it. This is also tinged with sadness as he wishes he'd addressed the feelings long ago so he could have actually enjoyed his career more.

Loosening the Grip

My dream and desire are to help people enjoy the journey of life instead of being hampered by fears. These fears are not invited; they slip in somehow and dominate thought patterns and behaviours. Speaking out such fears in therapy is so healing. The fraudulent client realised he *can* do it because he *has been* doing it, but an inbuilt defence mechanism has been working overtime. Defences kicking in during early life, as a result of detachment or trauma, hinder us if we do not take ourselves seriously in our thoughts and patterns. We find a way to manage because we are brilliantly and wonderfully made with such good inbuilt survival skills. This can make us driven and brilliant, but often at the expense of our emotional and physical health.

The sense of being a fraud can kick in at any time of life. Our internal voice that becomes our script and creates our way of being. I have known many people who have experienced panic attacks.

I have had a client say:
   'But I wasn't anxious at the time; I was just sitting with my friend.'

We press our anxiety down and think we have controlled it, but it rises up just when we relax or we hit a trigger point.

Even small adjustments can make significant waves that will impact the world around us. In our everyday lives and in business, our script which is our narrative is hugely important for our day-to-day work and for our outcomes.

▶ Will the business thrive or fail?

▶ Will it be a pleasure to be in?

We can change our narrative, but we first need to recognise it as it currently is, and then see the ripple effect as we make small or large changes.

Meeting a Dragon

Come with me on one of my 'wild adventures'!

We set off in my Toyota Rav4, not knowing what might happen. This particular event was a book launch that would bring about an unexpected adventure. This is how I like to live when I am really enjoying life and allowing myself to be free: I act on my instincts and see what happens.

So my colleague Malcolm and I set off to Manchester for the launch of *Teach Us to Pray* by Rob White. We had booked an Airbnb in Bakewell. We couldn't find it, as there was a big mansion in the way, so I called the owner of the Airbnb and was told to come through the gates of the big mansion – that *was* the Airbnb! To say we were in awe would be an understatement!

The following morning we were given a wonderful breakfast. I asked for the recipe of the porridge that Rachel, the owner, had served. She was setting up for a retreat, which inspired me as I got the impression she was on her own and was running all this as well as looking after five children. I wondered whether maybe I could do that too one day, as my dream was to run retreats.

Before we left, I felt we should give her a copy of Rob's book, so we did, and off we went.

A year later I was cooking my porridge thinking, 'I know I should be soaking it overnight and not cooking out the goodness, just as Rachel showed me.' But that morning I was preparing for The Business Show in London, and I was in a rush. I prayed, 'It looks like a great event. Please let me hear who I need to hear today and get back quickly as I have so much to do!'

Then one of the faces on the glossy cover of the brochure stood out. 'She looks familiar,' I thought, so I looked up her name and when she was speaking. She was a Dragon from *Dragons' Den*.

Her talk spoke straight into my heart. She spoke about how it's not all about fighting hard to get up the mountain, but we can take the scenic route up and enjoy the journey. It struck a chord with me, so afterwards we went to her stand.

Malcolm said to me, 'You have something to give to her.'
    I wanted to shout at him,
    'What on earth can I give a Dragon? Don't be so daft – who am I to be able to do that?'
    I stood there thinking, 'What have I got to give?!'
I began speak to this lady, when she stopped me and said, 'Sarah, you came to my house!'
    I was just about to say, 'You must have mistaken me for someone else.' My narrative, my old narrative was saying, 'No one remembers me or hears me.'
Then she added, 'You gave me a book, *Teach Us to Pray*.'

Oh my gosh!

I had to challenge myself and change my narrative. All this time she had remembered me and I had remembered her.

She told me that the book changed her life, and that of the hundreds of people who came through her home, she had remembered me.

So I had stayed at Rachel Elnaugh's house . . . really? She was the one who had given me her porridge recipe. I had thought of her so many times, how she had seemed so familiar – that lovely lady with the wonderful breakfast! I had always loved *Dragons' Den*, and even fancied myself as a little bit of an entrepreneur!

When I met her again at The Business Show, she invited me to stay with her again. I made myself do it as soon as I could, otherwise I would have talked myself out of it. I recognised that I needed to change my narrative. My old narrative of fear may have made me hesitate, so I just booked it up and went!

As I arrived, she said, 'Sarah, you are so supposed be here.'

'Why do you say that?' I asked.

'I prayed this prayer this morning,' she told me. 'Nothing happened, but I think you will be able to help me.' She showed me the prayer she had prayed. It was a prayer of forgiveness.

I put my case down and said, 'Can I tell you what happened when I prayed that prayer?' I went on to share my testimony of seeing Jesus face to face. We were standing under a picture of Jesus on her wall, which was the same one I had on my wall at home, and it had been the reason we had given her a copy of *Teach Us to Pray* on our previous visit.

Rachel Elnaugh became my business mentor, but more about that later on.

Passion Killers

Not changing our narrative can kill our passion, yet passion is the lifeline of joy and hope. If we get stuck and are unable to make a conscious effort to listen to our narrative, we miss out, and others do too, because we end up staying in that place.

A client was telling me how his elderly parents feared replacing their front door. It had huge holes in it that the postman put the mail through, and the newspaper was delivered that way too, even on a cold Scottish morning. It occurred to me that in their minds they were still living in a time of making do rather than spending any money. At the age of nearly ninety they were living in a cold house with holes in that threatened their health and even their lives.

How sad that they stayed there in fear and were not living for the moment. It would have made their family happier, too, if they had spent money on a new front door, so that they would not be worrying about them. (The family appeared quite wealthy.)

So what incorrect paradigms are playing out in your life, and where is the renewal of your mind that is needed? It's like a hummingbird thinking it's a fish, trying to swim and fit in with the sea creatures and never actually flying! It was designed for so much more – and so are you!

Solitary Tear

Emotional damage can lead to a 'cave' scenario, a solitary, reclusive existence where we cut ourselves off and try to live alone. Yet we are designed for communication, to connect and have communion.

During the coronavirus lockdown we were forced to do this for some time. We saw on the news, down our streets and in our own lives the damaging effects of having to cut ourselves off from others.

However, we have the advantage in this twenty-first century of being able to connect online as we have learnt so well through lockdown times. The damage can be limited and even give us a new platform to heal this pain and believe in fully living.

Flying High

So what would fully living look like and feel like for you? What would help you to be peaceful within your soul and spirit?

For me, being with family, doing the simplest of things gives me that peace. However, climbing a mountain and reflecting on the journey and the expanse also gives me great joy. On two occasions I have been fortunate enough to have been up in a helicopter; it made me feel so alive and ecstatic with joy. I was privileged to fly over Sydney with my brother Steven for a joint birthday treat.

I had saved some money with the intention of using it on a helicopter trip while travelling in my twenties, but I had never done it. A number of times while I was travelling I thought,
    'This would be the perfect place, but what if a better opportunity comes along later?'

So I waited, and I came back with the money. Having travelled around the world and returned, this was my one regret. I was still looking for that opportunity and I am thankful to have been able to share it with my brother.

Funnily enough, I do not like heights, so I was very nervous. In addition, I had a fear of flying. This rational fear of losing my life had kicked in once I had children. My instinct to be there for my children took over my rational thinking, as fear rose up to stop me risking my life. Now I wanted to overcome this and so I saw the link of my strong mothering instinct and how I needed to push through and get this flight booked. I felt the fear as I climbed in and decided to turn the adrenaline into excitement rather than let it take over.

As you can see from the photo of me smiling from ear to ear, it was amazing! I felt safe inside the helicopter and trusted the pilot, and that allowed me to feel free.

To have the opportunity to do this again over Niagara Falls was so exhilarating! I was in America on a work trip when my stepfather was taken ill. I was heading to Toronto and wasn't sure if I needed to fly back.

Malcolm and I arrived in Niagara and wondered how we could see it all quickly just in case I needed to fly home. We saw the helicopter pad and within ten minutes we were flying over the immensely powerful falls.

It was breathtaking. It was difficult to talk in the helicopter as it was so noisy. I wanted to say so much about how I was feeling, but then I realised it was best to just take it all in. Looking out for miles gave me a high level of joy. Of course, this was a once-in-a-lifetime experience.

But how can I find an inner calm and peace in my everyday? Working out my dreams, desires and needs, and helping others around me gives me that peace. I feel centred, joyful and encouraged, which leads me to want to impart more to others, giving me an even greater joy and peace.

I am wondering whether you don't allow yourself to dream any more, perhaps because you do not want to set yourself up to fail. This is an example of fear as a liar, and it has taken over in your mind. What was designed to protect you has become bad for you.

Switch On Your Brain

We remember from the previous chapter the importance of exercising your true grit. To quote Caroline Leaf, author of *Switch On Your Brain* and many other titles:

> The happiest people are not those with lots of nice things or lots of likes on social media; these, of course, can help make life more comfortable, but they do not guarantee true happiness. Rather, lasting happiness comes from something deep within us, from our character: it is an internal joy and peace that allows us to appreciate the small things and the big things, a mental strength and steadfastness that helps us get through the hard times and still smile. It is the ability to embrace the good and bad, and learn equally from both.[3]

---

[3] Caroline Leaf, *Switch On Your Brain: The Key to Peak Happiness, Thinking, and Health* (Grand Rapids: Baker Books, 2013),

It is about finding what helps you connect with others: a coffee, a lunch or doing something nice together; taking time with others, hearing their stories. Taking time out to calm our minds is good, as is learning something new about the world around us.

Gracelets

The past does influence our present and our future, but if we stop and take a look at the effects, we can then change our way of being. We can change the narrative by listening to the thoughts we have and being aware of them, and then, as we understand them, we have power over them.

What is the thing you would most like to change? Doing the same thing brings about the same result; using the same recipe will produce the same cake. This is a good opportunity to change something in your life for the better. Talk to others about your blind spots; others are usually happy to tell us!

> But who can discern their own errors?
> Forgive my hidden faults.
> *Psalm 19:12*

As we think and believe in our hearts, so we shall be. Let's search our hearts and discover what we really are believing. I was intrigued by the word *exousia*, meaning 'the right to act'. We all have that, so let's use it now. Let's act to make our lives more real and to hide less behind the person we have created to survive.

Those around you, including God, want you to start living your dream! Push it down into the screen of your heart – that's where things come into being. Speak it out and live it. Every good thing in the world was just once an idea, then it had to be put into being.

Your Ripple

Do you feel you have a false self that manifests itself when you are under stress?

Do you suffer from imposter syndrome?

Would you like to live more freely?

Is the ripple of worry and stress affecting your health, and are you stuck somewhere or somehow?

What stops you moving forward? What fears keep you stuck?

What is your biggest fear, irrational or not?

Maybe you have settled for less than the best, because you have not allowed yourself to conceive, perceive and believe for more in your heart first.

As the world changed around you during the coronavirus pandemic, what was your response to it?

Do you feel differently about yourself now?

Chapter 4

Feeling Not Filling

I love my role as a therapist, helping people to work things through. It's a privilege to journey with someone, to create a safe place and hold them in mind, like a mother does for a child. I have been told it is like being rocked gently, which is comforting and sweet. I facilitate this place and, when I see the need, I help clients travel to a deeper place while keeping the environment safe to explore the deepest parts of their hearts.

I believe each client holds the key to their own healing. It can't be rushed; it takes as long as it takes. It's important to allow a place to feel; no filling, just *feeling* what is coming up. I often sense something myself; I may feel suddenly heavy or sad, anxious or curious, so I share this to see whether a connection is made. What a privilege to be allowed into that inner sanctum of someone's soul, a unique being I can really and wholly see. To be seen, not having to hide, and to be heard is also a privilege in this busy and sometimes impersonal world.

▸ When were you last really seen by
  someone for who you are?
▸ When did you last feel that you were totally the
  centre of someone's world, truly heard and seen?

Some leave the journey before they reach the final step. They wonder, 'What will I feel or be without this pain? Who will I be?'

You will be you, with a sense of feeling whole, and things will simultaneously change around you. I have faith in the process, and I can express how fantastic it is when a client has a penny-dropping moment or looks back to see how far they have come. It's worth the risk of the unknown and going on till the end. But for some, the fear is so real it deceives even the most educated and clever of people. How clever we can be to deceive ourselves.

Fear is a great deceiver: False Evidence Appearing Real. What lies on the other side is the person you were meant to be, with added strength and understanding that can only come by learning through the pain.

During my training as a psychotherapist I was asked many times,
   'How are you feeling about that?'

First of all, I thought,
   'Well, isn't it obvious?'

Apparently not, because I was supposed to say it, to hear myself speak out my feelings and own them. It took a while, but I soon got into the flow. I realised in one session that I had felt loneliness for the first time during my teenage years. There had been no time or room for loneliness in our busy home, so when it hit I remember thinking,
   'What on earth is that feeling deep in my stomach?'

It was not at all pleasant and I tried to avoid it from then on. I entered into a pattern of being busy so I could avoid that feeling. My stepdad nicknamed me Flash, as I would always be flashing in and out.

My middle name is Melanie and I loved singing, so he also called me Melody. I now wonder whether I sang to block out my thoughts while I was standing still.

Bundle of Emotions

This brings me to explore how we are not growing up to be emotionally healthy adults in the twenty-first century. We need to discover our feelings, name them, recognise them and embrace, tolerate or accept them. If we do not know what the feelings are, we have nothing to pin a name to or recognise, and when they rise up we are left with a bundle of emotions that we were born with.

That's how we are born. Observe a baby: cute, small, adorable, noisy, vulnerable and so on. When they don't sleep or stop crying it makes me smile and say to God,
    'Ahh, that's why you made babies so cute – so that their parents love them instantly!'
    If we had to work on the parent–child relationship in the way we do with other relationships, the human race would be extinct!

So this bundle of emotions – that's you or me – has been born into this world, and we soon learn how to manage the environment around us. We cry, and food appears; wow, that's great! But what if it doesn't appear? Crisis; going to die soon if someone doesn't do something. If you've ever heard that newborn cry, every nerve and instinct wants to shout back, 'I'm coming!' even if the baby isn't yours!

As that bundle of emotions grew up, you discovered that floors are hard and so are table edges.

Bikes are great, but knees are soft. Clothes must be mastered and conquered – oh, let's make it really interesting and add laces!

The world of a baby or a child is cold, warm, sweaty, irritating, funny and scary, to name just a few feelings and emotions. Our feelings have kept us alive and they make us human.

Sauna Inspiration – Spain

Letting go of control, surrendering and submitting, all get blocked by fear of losing control and not being able to get it back. What does that look like? We all fear something, and it holds us back in our everyday life, our whole life, but it can change in our focus as we look at it.

Ultimately – in a very direct way of looking at it – we fear dying. We fear losing everything, and this plays out in our everyday. We fear letting go of the control we have, control we gained during our early years. When we were dependent, we had to cry to evoke a reaction from our mother to feed us and to meet our every need. When these needs are not met, we learn to adapt, and as there is no perfect parent, something will inevitably be missed. We create defence mechanisms to cope, to avoid rejection at a deep level. These are not conscious thoughts, but deep in our being we adjust to unmet needs.

We are simple beings yet our needs are complex, because as things go wrong and we adapt, we create a new view of the world. The world around us keeps changing, so we keep changing to adapt to it. Changes in our perception start to develop, and they distort or enhance our view. Fears created at this point – or any point in childhood – then can set the course of our life.

Existing with these limitations that are unseen and unknown keep us from knowing ourselves more fully. Fears block us from truly knowing ourselves and living in a more fulfilled way, knowing our gifts and calling. Knowing what our fears are – speaking them out, writing them down, addressing them head on – releases the power of them over us, and we are empowered. No matter how silly, small, large, frightening, unreal, unrealistic these fears might be, they are there and they dominate our everyday.

When I'm in a sauna, I'm sometimes just about to drop off to sleep, but then I pull myself back as I am aware that this is not the best environment to sleep in. I have the power to pull myself back; I can control the situation. This led me to think about that moment before we go to sleep at night, and how we surrender every day to letting go and being still.

It is almost like being in between two worlds, a sense of slowly dropping off, I experience such lightness and freedom.
On a flight I saw remarkable cloud formations which illustrates this beautifully, the space between the two.

If we are fearful this phase before sleep can be disturbed Untangling our fears and identifying anxiety is good for us, but we also need to recognise when it is too much and not good for us. Stress is part of this: good stress drives us, but too much overwhelming, negative stress is harmful to our mind and bodies.

We need to begin to allow ourselves to feel, rather than fill our time because we need to push away our feelings, which is something we may well have learnt from a young age. When we are young, we are encouraged to occupy ourselves to keep us from getting bored or into trouble. This created pattern is there to help, yet it can become something of a hindrance.

Meditation, perhaps out in nature, on a piece of writing or a verse from the Bible, is a good approach to finding this space.

This is good for our bodies and minds and brings them into alignment where we can hear, read and feel as a whole. Pilates does something similar for me, helping me to focus on my body movement, taking me out of thinking and retuning me with my body. This helps relax my mind and then I am more open to awareness of ourselves.

Any activity will help us in this way as we release endorphins and burn up hormones. All this helps us to be more in tune with ourselves, if we keep it in moderation. Gym bunnies (people who spend a lot of time exercising in the gym) may take it too far, so it becomes about the image and performance. Once again, an example of a good thing going too far and becoming not so good for us.

Gaming No Longer Playing

Gaming can be a danger to young people's minds and their ability to communicate beyond their gaming friends. It can be a way to cut themselves off from reality. Many games these days are violent and fast moving. Hours of gaming can change the way the mind is wired, and it then becomes difficult to even focus on a meal, a sibling or a family event.

Being aware of this and monitoring the games that are being played could help. My wonderful godson Cam decided at the age of fourteen not to play Fortnite because he saw how angry his friends became when they played it. It is hard for those playing to see change in themselves, but others watching can see it and feel it.

This is the ultimate filling up of the mind. It takes over time and body, as the body will react as if the situation in the game is real.

I have known many parents send their sons for counselling to help these young victims of their own fun come back into the real world of family life. One boy, acknowledging the influence it had on him, asked his grandmother to take away his console while he studied. He would get a bus to her house, have tea with her and then play for an hour as a treat once he had finished his work. What a wise move! Removing what distracts is a big step, but the first and biggest of all is to see it.

I will offer some more thoughts on gaming in chapter 10, 'A Contagious Ripple', if you care to stay with me on this journey till then . . .

Human Beings Are Meant to 'Be'

We humans need to learn how to 'be'. As we are 'human beings', surely this should be straightforward. Feelings are meant to be felt, not feared. Finding ourselves in the feelings and learning more about ourselves and others is surely the name of the game. Otherwise why are we here?

My children used to catch me out if I said the word 'do' and then 'do' immediately after. They would burst out,
    'You did a do-do!'

To be busy 'doing' all day, then to get up to 'do' another day ... Doing so much surely only creates 'do-dos' so we then have more to clear up!

This led me to think about all the things I am doing. Yes, we need to achieve, and it feels good to be active, but let's take this reminder to be present in the moment; to be enjoying what we can, actively aware of ourselves, our thoughts and our feelings as we journey through the day.

Even in periods of forced inactivity, such as the recent lockdown period, we may well be keeping ourselves far too busy. We want to avoid boredom and facing any emotions or thoughts that may come up. I am aware of the extremes this period has created in our society. Many are left doing nothing, while others are rushed off their feet. The 'haves' and the 'have-nots' financially sit far apart, and now we are seeing the same with time.

It's wonderful that many people have given time and energy to the NHS and started a completely different role in life.

Yet many cannot give this time and have had to find a new routine fairly quickly. Many different online ways of filling time suddenly came into being as a new norm was enforced.

Creatively, we seem to have coped remarkably well in many ways, but are we allowing ourselves to embrace the pause we have been granted? A time when the world is on pause is a good time to stop and be with yourself rather than finding a new busy schedule that just replaces the old one.

Let's slow down and enjoy the moments we have, as, sadly, too many lives are cut short. Even if they are not cut short, why be unfortunate enough to get to the age of eighty to find we were too busy 'doing' to really enjoy or remember many of the moments. We can be geared so wholeheartedly towards big events in life that we miss the wonderful, small moments of connecting. Eventually we realise that it was the small moments that were the big moments after all. Be glad at the end of your time to say,

'I did it well, I was there, I was present and I enjoyed life.'

A sporting legend once told me he wished he had enjoyed his career more at the time. He regretted the fact that he had stressed over each match and worried over each loss, and he wished he had celebrated the wins more. Allowing ourselves to do this is probably the hardest, yet it is the most privileged, way of living. Can we allow ourselves this privilege? If you were going to give a gift to a friend, would this not be the best gift you can give – the here and now?

Can we give ourselves this?

When we are walking more in the here and now, we can gain strength which allows us to manage more than we would ever believe possible, no longer restricted by fear.

Grace Theatre Company

My daughter has surprised me in this many times. She will face a fear head on, almost bullishly, if that's the right word. As an actress, she wants constructive feedback, otherwise she sees it as a waste of time. She gave up on training, telling the tutor,

'My mum could have told me I did well; I need more than that. What can I do better?'

So I introduced her to Mal Corden, James Corden's dad, hoping he would talk some sense into her and she would go back to training. Instead he told us that, after they had scrimped and saved to get James to training college, he quit, as he wasn't learning from it. James had been born with the talent and motivation to follow his gifting. This wasn't the encouragement I was actually looking for from Mal but I could see the sense. I had to laugh!

Nicole worked really hard and created Grace Theatre Company. She produced a show in Marylebone, London, to showcase a particular writer's work. She worked hard for weeks to create the scenery, choose the scripts, put funding in place, book the theatre, audition actors and produce tickets, fliers and online marketing. There was a flurry of excitement, yet she was nervous about bringing it all together.

On the night we saw a great show, written by Jenny Webb from Los Angeles, which represented many aspects of life that are often hard to discuss.

All the work behind the scenes was done, and we got to see a fresh yet raw performance, as if it were the only time it would happen.

I am sharing this with you to demonstrate the link between behind-the-scenes work and needing to be in the moment. It took time and a lot of hard work to bring this show together. In life, we also need to give ourselves time to bring the show together. Yet real life is not a performance; it's more about being in the moment and enjoying life. Unpacking our emotions is the hard work behind the scenes that brings the joy of being in the moment of everyday life.

Wearing Our Fear

We might choose not to go there, convincing ourselves that no one else can see the anxiety and fear we are holding. Hold on to your hat, because you might be shocked to hear that others probably sense it, see it and hear it already. Even the greatest of leaders share such stories.

The secretary of a Christian leader told him she knew when he was stressed; they all felt it.

She asked him why he didn't share it with his team so they could help? He thought he had hidden it really well. The leader shared this with a friend, who said,
   'Yep, buddy, we all can tell when you're stressed.'

He was shocked, but then went and sought some professional help.

A personal experience illustrates this well. On one of my walks with my lovely two Rough Collies, Bella and Charlie, I was picking wild blackberries. One of the berries squashed between my fingers and juice ran down my leg. It looked as though I had been stabbed!

We can believe we are hiding the pain, but it's still there and others can see it. If it were as visible as the berry juice, we would all do something about it rather fast. I couldn't get home quick enough to wash myself, as it looked gruesome. But we can get used to things very easily and sooner or later we stop noticing them, and they then become the norm. This can then affect our identity as they become a part of us.

Joining the Club

I am blessed to be a member of a luxurious, newly built spa. I see the visually pleasing, purpose-built spa from a lounge to outside, creating the perfect relaxation area. The blend of lights, colour, smells, music and cleanliness are exquisite and wonderfully overwhelming. The club has been perfectly designed for its members to relax. It has been done beautifully, and I am privileged to be able to visit this wonderful place. I marvel at the stonework, plants, water cascading. . . need I go on?!

My point is that we can have things wonderfully lined up and they work seamlessly when they are purposefully made. As we find our purpose and work to our calling, we can begin to feel that seamlessness that has been missing all along.

When things go wrong, which they inevitably will and have done, the brakes go on and our flow is lost.

The coronavirus did that to us all. When this happens early in life, it sets us up in the wrong way, as we have looked at, and if we haven't learnt how to put ourselves back on track, this creates a pile-up. The emotions get stuck, we block our hearts and can sense that something is wrong. Given the time to talk, as we have been designed to do, we can work through the block and begin to heal. Alternatively, we might ignore our emotions and our spiritual senses and strive on in the hope that in time it will go away. It does for a while, but it's still there under the surface. Sometimes it leaks out in a comment or attitude that shocks us, let alone the person on the receiving end.

So I offer you a time of stopping to *feel* what is coming up for you. It may be something that you have not heard before, or it could be that same old thought. That's OK. We can stay here for a little while and explore it. The fear is that it will take over and never leave. The truth is that it *will* take over and never leave if it isn't dealt with it. It can be a self-fulfilling prophecy – what we fear the most comes back to bite you on the butt.

Now is the time to start feeling, even if it is hard to experience what is coming up. I hope you will be able to make the most of the time the world has given us to pause and learn from the opportunity. Take time with a counsellor or talk to someone who will listen without shutting you down. There is too much of this in the world. We need a safe space to share the darkest parts of our hearts so that we can live more freely in the here and now.

Right Side of the Grass

Having breakfast in a hotel in America, I heard one of the servers ask a customer,

'How are you doing today?' I got the impression he was a regular customer.

His response stopped me in my tracks:
   'I'm still on the right side of the grass, so that's got to be a good day, right?'

I nearly called this book *Right Side of the Grass*, but maybe that'll be my next one!

While we still have time on this earth to make a difference – to feel, see, taste, be and share – we are still on the right side of the grass, and we can make a difference. I found it interesting to discover that many of the younger people I met who had contracted coronavirus lost their sense of taste and smell. I wondered whether this was a generational thing – losing the appetite and taste for life. We need this to keep aiming for our goals to keep positive.

Older people who catch coronavirus appear to be more at risk of losing the battle to breathe. Many, sadly, lost their ability to fight, perhaps because of too many fights they had already been through and their bodies therefore struggled to beat the virus.

Needs Met By Far!

Another story that unfolded before my daughter and me, reminded me how we can make a difference, especially if we are open to what comes towards us – or even to trying to find something for ourselves.

My daughter wanted to go surfing, to have a break from London and do a sport she loved. I said,

'Find the surf and we'll find a way.'

She found the ideal spot in Cascais in Portugal. I wanted to book a very nice-looking hotel, but my daughter said she would feel more comfortable walking through with a surfboard at the one next door. Nothing too fancy; just comfortable. I had really wanted to spoil us and have a bit of luxury as we had both been through a lot and I felt we needed a treat. But I reluctantly booked the cheaper hotel next door.

So off we went for a five-day break. When we arrived, the hotel pulled out all the stops to supply my gluten-free food. The owner, a gentleman in his eighties, had been entertaining for years and still enjoyed a drink with the guests. He turned up each night with a new favourite drink for us. We were totally blessed with a comfortable room, a view of the sea and all our needs taken care of, and so much more!

I realised from this experience that sometimes we think we need something, yet being open to other things can bring even greater blessings. We visited the other hotel one evening for a special meal. It was lovely, but overpriced and not at all relaxing. We didn't feel taken care of in a relaxed way; more that it was a duty to assist us. We were very happy to return to our comfortable, more homely, relaxed and friendly hotel. We had made friends there; we felt looked after and had a connection with the staff.

If I had pushed to be spoilt in the posh hotel we may not have actually had a treat at all. We did not have second best; we were treated with care and given attention for who we were.

The owner loved to hear about my daughter's acting career and told us about all the other actors, prime ministers and entrepreneurs who had visited over the years. We were in the right place at the right time; just perfect for what we needed.

Someone Out There?

So let's start talking about our feelings and start living while we are on the right side of the grass. If I share my heart a little more, maybe you will find it easier to share your own.

One of my fears has been not knowing whether there is someone out there for me. I am not talking necessarily about a partner but someone who loves me and is there for me. I have realised over time that this is because my real father was not a part of my life when I was young. Although I had a stepfather, I felt I needed to find my biological father, then everything would be OK.

Finding him when I was forty years old was amazing; it answered many of my questions and I even found other family members. How fantastic to gain so much and to enjoy time with them. We all benefited, and it was one of the bravest and best things I have ever done.

I thought about that sense of needing someone, someone who thinks of me, who wants to know I'm doing all right. This feeling pulled at my heart. I knew I was doing well, and I was happy, so why did I keep feeling like this?

I studied a little bit of neuroscience and learnt that I had rewired my brain this way.

I was used to this thought, this feeling. Finding someone to fill it, even the right person – my dad – didn't stop my brain from going there.

I worked on a mental/emotional detox which takes 21 days (more about this later). Each day for 21 days I worked on this thought and I have felt a real peace since. It took me three lots of 21 days to really start to feel the difference, but it has been life-changing. I am happier in the moment and enjoying life; I'm actually a little nervous that I may become lazy and do nothing, as I am so able to just be!

So back to you and being brave. Tears should be allowed, perhaps even compulsory, when working through this book, as healing needs to happen in all our lives. We may have had a good upbringing, but we have all lived through disappointments and losses we may not have reconciled with.

Allowing tears leads to hope in the solitude, and then it leads us back to ourselves and others. Discord can be caused by disharmony, so we need to get back into perfect order, talk out the negative and work to make things right and bring back the harmony.

You may have gone through trauma, as I have. Trauma leads to many changes in life. Getting back to order, love, honesty and obedience to our calling can result in power and success. Not worldly power to control others, but power to lead you to your true calling, your true way of being that you may not have even known before the trauma. Nothing is wasted; all will be used for good if we can find the energy, true grit and passion to see us through. The alternative is to give up and let go, but I know what I would rather see you do.

Totally Motivation Matters

To lighten the mood a little, let me introduce my friend Wendy H. Jones, author, speaker and member of many committees.

Wendy is very good at living life to the full. With so much favour on her life, it is contagious. I have been described like that too, but I found it hard to see myself that way. Then I met Wendy and thought,

'Is this what people see when they see me?'

If that is the case, I must embrace it and run with it, as it's a gift not to be ignored! We started to work together and from an idea to existence came *Bertie the Buffalo*, a chidrens' true story book that endeavours to pull everyone's hearts.

I was thrilled to get to know and spend time with Wendy, who gave me a copy of her book, *Motivation Matters*, which offers tips to writers. I am thankful to Wendy for many things, including for this timely book. As I read it, it occurred to me why we got on so well: she was saying much of what I wanted to say about being kind to ourselves and enjoying the processes of life and of writing. I had begun to be so absorbed by my writing that I was losing the sense of fun in the journey, so this was a good reminder.

I was definitely losing my joy, as the stress began to build each day:

'Can the world go away. . . Aarrhh, don't they know I have a deadline?!'

I was so wound up by life happening around me that I left my office and headed to the pool. Sitting by it – exercise can wait – I turned to Wendy's book and read exactly what I needed to do: step away from the writing, exercise, smell the roses, as my stepdad would tell me, and get back into the moment.

This is something that my wonderful Collies can help me do as we walk in the fields and the sunshine. I had done that earlier in the day, so reading about it in Wendy's book was a timely reminder. Sometimes we just need to be reminded to be kind to ourselves.

So, as Wendy says, we need to step away occasionally, take a day off, take exercise, take walks, enjoy music and take photos. It's like she has been stalking me! I love those things and I found that they kept me sane while I was going through trauma, and so I had naturally developed this as part of my writing programme. I suggest the same to my clients, nudging them towards self-care and encouraging them to allow time for pleasure. This can be hard to plan into our schedule, especially for parents, but once we do it, we wonder how we managed before.

Wendy talks of releasing the inner artist. This is something I encourage counselling clients to do when I sense they are stuck emotionally. So often the voice of fear creeps in: 'I wasn't good at art at school. . .' Yet as I guide them, they tap into areas they didn't know were there. I have had a sixty-year-old man sobbing with relief as we uncovered hidden depths, just through using coloured pens and paper.

Interestingly, Wendy goes on to talk about water, and here I am by the pool desperately wanting to keep writing but instead am watching the ripples of the water settle. I had an amazing epiphany some time ago that just spoke straight into my heart and inspired the cover. I would like to share this with you.

Reflecting On Our Ripple

I love the moment of getting into water when it is completely still and seeing the ripple it makes across the rest of the pool. I watch the ripple closely and see other ripples dancing upon it, smaller and going in different directions. I am completely in the moment. I could stay here forever.

Then someone gets in and I have to adjust to sharing the space, as my ripple hits theirs. I sense the swim getting harder; I feel the resistance, but I keep going. I realise that others' ripples make us work harder. We are not alone in the world;

we wouldn't last long that way. We need each other and each other's ripples to shape us, sharpen us and enable us to experience life to the full.

This I used to struggle with. 'Why does it have to be hard?' I have kept asking, especially when these ripples have been negative, such as times of being bullied or even abused. Yet we can use these times to learn and grow stronger, once we have come to terms with the initial feelings of vulnerability and shock. It's what we do with it all that matters, and if we can stay with learning from it, for ourselves and others, we will keep growing, remain teachable and keep learning.

Learning about ourselves and being open to learning about others is a gift. Being compassionate and understanding a situation from another point of view helps both them and us.

We need to fully understand the word 'compassion': if we were to fully take on that others' hurts are our hurts, would we treat others differently? Within church communities we say that when one person hurts, it's like a part of the body hurting. We are not separate; it affects the rest of the body. If we were to see this in the whole of life and the wider community, would we care more?

This image made me think, if we really totally believed what is done here is reflected in heaven would we still remain the same?

Let's just look at the word 'compassion': 'com' is to be with. To sit with another's pain is compassion. It is hard to do; we want to avoid our own pain, so looking at others' pain can be too hard and close.

However, if we do help others to work through theirs, they grow stronger and more able to help you or others in turn. The ripple can come back around as a positive. Can we live like this, paying it forward?

The Woodman

I had a client who found it so difficult to cope that he kept heading to the woods to hide, until one day he didn't come home. He lived in the woods for a year, making his home with a tent and a fire. He felt so damaged that he became a solitary being, until he was brought out of the woods again by his family.

We worked together in many creative ways to bring this man back into community living. He had great talent and yet no self-belief. He could not walk down the road for fear of others' thoughts about him.

One day I asked him, 'What are they thinking of you?'

He replied, 'They might laugh or think I'm weird.'

'You know, they're probably thinking more about themselves, just as you are.'

After a while he was able to walk down the road, and then over time he could catch a train and a bus. He learnt to be in the here and now of a moment rather than in his head, which he had learnt to do as a result of being bullied in school. He had a passion for working with wood and eventually carved out a career in woodwork and became independent.

What a privilege to journey with this guy! It was not easy, or fast, but seeing small changes was enough to stay on the journey with him. As I believed in him, he began to believe in himself. His ripple entailed beautifully created wooden articles that blessed others. As we looked at his woodwork, he would point out the imperfections, but I would see them as adding character to the art. He began to see his imperfections as assets too. His ripple meeting others wasn't so bad after all.

The ripple in a pool meets the edge and comes back again, and the good ripple we send out comes back to us. We learnt this together as we watched his woodwork become gifts for others. It touched his heart that someone would value what he could do so naturally. Finding our natural talents and sharing them with others should be the most natural process, yet self-esteem and lack of value in ourselves steals this away from us.

If you feel encouraged by this story then please stop and think about what your own talents are. I will ask this again in the Gracelets at the end of the chapter.

Right Place, Right Time

This is a belief I have learnt to turn into a prayer since I realised how my life could have been cut short in my late teens. This has put me in good stead, as I hope to meet the right people and enjoy many good moments with people. However, I did not realise until writing this book that I still held fear about that event; uncovering it has released me even more to live in the moment.

As a teenager, I had narrowly missed being blown up by an IRA bomb by an ATM at a bank in St Albans. I could not find a parking space, so I drove on to meet some friends. Just ten minutes later the bomb exploded in a building nearby that I didn't realise my mother was in. She had no idea I would have been at the ATM itself if I had been able to park the car. We exchanged stories the next day and both realised how close it had been for us both.

In addition, my eldest stepbrother went to Northern Ireland during his career in the armed forces. I am much younger than him and I was fearful that he would not return home. He did and all was well, apart from shrapnel wounds he was fine, so I guess I squashed the fear as I never spoke about it.

I recently went to Ireland for a conference; it was a time for healing of relationships between the Irish, French, Germans and English. Other nationalities were there too, so it was a momentous gathering. During this conference, I felt fear lift off me and I found myself free to dance. Not quite the Irish jig, but my own expression of dance! As I danced, I felt free.

I enjoyed the time and returned home feeling younger and lighter. The fear of humanity had gone and I saw how the fear of Ireland and the Irish had crept in when I was younger.

To have the fear lifted that had been there for decades, as I had held it unknowingly, was such a relief. A relief even though I had not known it was there – how strange. But this demonstrates what I am writing about – freedom in the now having let out the emotions that were buried so deep I had missed them.

Emerging Patterns

How many people can we think of for whom we see patterns that affect their lives day in day out? It's very easy to talk to someone outside the situation about it, yet to go to the person themselves and approach it is very difficult. Sometimes it would be helpful to be brave, to approach the person and say,

'Look, I say this in love as this is affecting your life and ours too . . .'

In an organisation, it may be easier to avoid such people. Yet we all think we are doing well to cover up, but are we?

Let's stop for a moment . . .

Think about one person you could consider having this conversation with. Then think about whether there is something in your life that someone might raise with you.

So many people live by over-compensating in order to fit in. This is also known as living within the adapted/false self as mentioned previously. They don't feel understood and they don't know how to have their needs facilitated.

What can we do about that?

The first step is to take the lid off these issues and start to allow ourselves to be vulnerable, so that we can be available to help others.

Balcony Moment

I was at a women's conference at Green Pastures Church in Northern Ireland. The church had a balcony, so I went up to take a look.

There were a couple of ladies up there, and then the pastor, Jeff Wright, came in.

'Sorry, ladies,' he said, 'but we are keeping this closed as we would like everyone downstairs together today.'

'Sorry, Jeff, but would you mind if I pointed something out?'

'Sure.'

'Sometimes we just need this balcony moment, I have been there myself, needing to be away from everyone and be with God'

Jeff instantly apologised and allowed the ladies to stay. I was so impressed that he could hear me and act so instantly with compassion. He had created a safe space.

Sometimes it is hard to be around others, and a little time out is probably all we need. I have seen that when people are going through mental health issues or emotional challenges, they want to be with people but find it hard to actually be among them. They may just need to connect with God, and a balcony is a perfect place for this in a church.

Gracelets

I'm like my Dad . . .

I believe we are created in God's likeness, so we all have some kind of creative ability. Through our life experiences we are moulded by our thinking, so our brains are tuned in a certain way. When we experience deprivation and trauma, these affect our brains. They can cause blockages, and yet if we push through we can find creative ways to manage the stress. For many people, the coronavirus offered them that opportunity – many were surprised by the creativity they discovered within themselves or within others!

We each have individual gifts; I cannot be you and you cannot be me. So, like the Woodman, we need to come out of the forest and find our thing, and we will then all benefit.

I was listening to a song on the radio called 'Paparazzi'.[4] It held my attention as I thought about the photographer taking photos of celebrities going about their business. Then I broke down the word, and I saw it differently: *Papa – at – see*.

- ► *Papa* looking down on us, with his main aim being to see us.
- ► *at see* – seeing us is his greatest pleasure, as a father would watch his children.

I believe God wants to see us happy and enjoying the moment. Hold that thought – God our Father, our Papa, enjoying the moment of us enjoying the moment.

---

4 Lady Gaga, 'Paparazzi' (2008).

What a treasure and a gift! Let's have many of these moments with him and with our family, friends and colleagues as we learn to share our gifts.

Starting to feel, being in the moment rather than filling our time, can be challenging, as can staying with what comes up. We need to pray to see what God has for us, to help lighten the load. The plans he has for you are to prosper you, not to harm you (Jeremiah 29:11): this promise is for you. Reach out and grab it with both hands. Pray with someone else to have confirmation and keep stepping out into given opportunities until it becomes clear. God will give you the desires of your heart.

Disappointments from the past can get in the way, so facing those and moving forward can be painful. Yet it is time well spent; have open hands to receive what is before you. Easily said, I know, but let me remind you once again that you are not alone in this; we are journeying together. Your blessings are everyone's blessings; we are all in this together.

Meditation is spoken of in the Bible as a way of seeking God. It is not something to be fearful of as a bad practice, but is something we should seek out.

> The purposes of a person's heart are deep waters,
> but one who has insight draws them out.
> *Proverbs 20:5*

As we stay in the moment and allow the feelings to come through, it creates space for new dreams and desires – either those that have been buried or those not yet born.

Just a reminder to allow tears – these can lead to hope in the solitude, when we take time out alone. Then they lead us back to ourselves and others.

Discord can be caused by disharmony, so we need to get back into perfect order, talk out the negative and work to make things right.

Your Ripple

What would a safe place look like for you to be able to start feeling, not filling, your time?

What brave move could you make to allow this time?

Would you like to give your friends and family the gift of being in the moment?

Can you gift yourself the same, of being in the here and now?

Take a moment to note down what has come up as you have read this chapter, then ask yourself what feelings might be pushed down by the filling up of your time.

What are you doing to fill your time? What could you let go of?

Has something come up that needs facing? What would help you do that?

As you stay in the moment and allow the feelings to come through, are there new dreams and desires that have been buried or have not been born yet?

Remember the ripple effect: being in the moment allows another to be there with you.

Chapter 5

The Swift and the Butterfly

Comparisons and Competition

I consider a fabulous tree that has been growing for years. I see it before me from the warmth of an outside pool. It is autumn; the leaves are just turning and the sun is shining through them. The sun breaks through the different aspects of the tree, showing the many angles of the larger branches, leaves, twig-like endings, thin branches and thicker winding ones that lead to the huge trunk. All its majestic being is there on many levels: beauty, strength, uprightness, swaying yet firm. It's a marvel to watch with the autumn shadows moving around.

I consider this tree for a while – it's a tree being a tree.
   No complications with its roots.
   It's been planted where it is.
   It hasn't been contaminated by other trees.
   It stands majestically.
   It just keeps being its true self and growing through the years to its full height and potential.
   It never questions whether it is in the right place; it knows it's a tree.
   It doesn't fight the other trees or challenge the season changes; it just goes with the flow.
   It blows with the wind and does not fight against it or the elements around it.

If we could be more like that tree, knowing who we are and why we are where we are, swaying with the changes and fully coming into our full height and potential, that would be majestic too.

Being fully seen for who we are; no fear, just being ourselves, happy in our own skin like the tree in its bark.

Celebrating all we are.

A Treat to Retreat

I learnt a lesson running a retreat at Hirondelles in Central France with our kind retreat hosts Ian and Lucie Harvey. I was wearing a dress with birds on and as I arrived in France, I heard,
    'Well done with the swift dress, Sarah – you do realise that *hirondelle* means swift?!'

'They are swifts then? I was hoping they were!' I replied, wishing I could have been more purposeful and confident in my response!

So, in tune, or not, I was in the right place at the right time wearing the right dress, hooray! A member of our retreat then told me that her favourite bird was a swift, and it felt it was completely right that she was with us. She told me all she loved about swifts and how much more there was to them than butterflies. I was a little taken aback that we were comparing, and I had been planning to wear my butterfly dress the following day!

Thinking about this helped me focus on how easily we can defend what is close to our heart.

This lady was needing to bring herself into the retreat, to express herself, and may not have meant at all to belittle butterflies in comparison to swifts. I had to let it settle into my thinking how we can champion something so hard we can miss out on what others have to offer.

I looked at the swifts and saw their flight patterns, direct and graceful. I also watched butterflies and saw their gentleness and purpose of pollination. Flitting here and there may look frivolous and wasteful, yet they have great purpose too. Have you ever watched two or three fly around each other? It's like a dance. They know the steps as they twirl around each other incredibly closely.

How marvellous is the world of nature. Butterflies and swifts do not compete, so why should we? The swift is fast, purposeful and, as its name says, swift! We can appreciate both for their own beauty, and I do not need to protect or defend either.

Our own sense of keeping up and comparisons with others can be inbuilt from an early age. Being undiagnosed dyslexic set this course for me early on, as well as being the youngest of six and the only girl. I had no escape from comparisons and competition. I believed this left me not wanting to compete and switched off my competitive switch.

Looking back, I realise I was sporty and that would have been fed by competition. However, I see now that if I felt over-shadowed I would pull back and withdraw rather than stand firm. Seeing this pattern, I have had to learn to sense whether something is healthy competition or whether it is making my life miserable.

I have observed that I like to find people around me who are doing similar things, so that we can work together to be pacesetters for one another. This feels healthy and collaborative, which gives energy and hope.

I can visualise a bucket of crabs all grabbing on to each other. As one gets higher up the side of the bucket, another grabs it and pulls it down. There is no way out for any of them. To hand down a ladder and bring another on behind you is far more empowering.

Viewing the world from a competitive stance is learnt early with our siblings, as mentioned earlier. If we have a healthy view of this, we may have had a good role model of parenting and enjoyed being with our siblings. If this is the case, we would normally have been able to automatically figure this out in the world. Many, however, like myself, have experienced it to be challenging, so issues may have come up in friendships, in the family and so on. We can choose to explore these issues to see how they are playing out in our lives. Turning them around can be life-changing, rippling out to others, even if they do not necessarily acknowledge it. As I share this with clients, they start to see the effects of their changes, which boosts confidence and hope.

I would like to live in a world where we boost each other's confidence and learn to embrace the best in one another so that the ripple goes out to benefit us all. Is it selfish to wish that?

I have been in a relationship where I felt other women were baiting me, tempting me to compete with them emotionally and physically.

I began not to like my own reactions to this; anger and resentment were not feelings I was used to living with. I had to point out the competitive nature being placed upon me and I decided that if it didn't stop I had to walk away. I walked away and slowly became more at peace with myself again. I would rather be alone and work through my own issues than have others put upon me that which isn't mine. I had a fear of being alone until I realised we are never really alone; this is a state of mind.

Oh No! That FOMO

We can experience loneliness, believing everyone is out doing something wonderful in couples when we are alone of an evening. FOMO (fear of missing out) is real and strong. Yet in reality, the fear grows stronger because we give power to it. We might believe we are really missing out, but the reality is usually not what social media would have us believe. It is amazing how, even during a time of social distancing, we can still feel that others are meeting online while we are left out.

Social media sets us up: no matter how young or old, single or married, it can grip us. Stepping back from posts when you are home alone and taking time to read or listen to something that will feed your soul (keep reading this book) will be much more beneficial for your mental and emotional health. I have recently been about to post images of my holiday, but I paused to wonder who it was for. Was it,
    'Look at me!' or, 'You should try this place, it's great!'

Whatever the reason, I thought hard before posting anything and then decided to keep it very lean.

Showing my friends and family my pictures on my return was much more rewarding, because they then couldn't say,

'Yes, I saw that online,' which would have stolen the moment I could have shared with them.

This has also removed the risk that others might be jealous of my trips away. Facebook can be a face that we put on. Used well, it can be a great way of connecting with people all around the world. We can all suffer from jealousy and feel that we are competing with the world, perhaps try making changes to posts and watch how the ripple changes the course. It starts with us and comes back to us at the end of the day.

Intelligent Species

As I write, I can see a bird high up in an old oak tree. This place where I am writing was made for Lord Mountbatten, so this beautiful tree could be from his time here. It's huge in stature and the bird is sitting looking out across the fields. I marvel at the fact that human beings are the intelligent species, yet we can be so concerned about other things that we miss the view so much of the time. The bird will just be there, being a bird and taking in the view, perhaps considering its next meal, but still happy being a bird. We can learn so much from animals.

I have seen swans on Sandringham Estate and thought,

'Do you realise how privileged you are?'

Swans are happy just being, and are totally unaware that there are other birds scavenging in refuse tips.

We could let go and live life for what we can make of it, as we know there are always people less fortunate than ourselves.

We can even do more with that knowledge – we could step out and help those people too.

The Caterpillar and the Butterfly

As you will see from the cover of this book and my logo, I relate well to butterflies. This started to emerge as my life hit rock bottom and I had to build myself up again. I had to transform, or I felt I would die, give up, break down completely. Because of my love for my children, this wasn't an option, so I pushed in and pushed upwards. The trauma of living through many areas of deceit, betrayal, abuse and abandonment had to be used for something good.

During the writers' retreat in France, we went for a wonderful walk in the countryside. A caterpillar was hanging from a leaf in front of us. It left me thinking about the caterpillar, how it may die during the metamorphosis, but this is a natural occurrence and it just keeps doing its thing. When the time is right it will emerge as a beautiful butterfly, vibrant and alive. The process can't be rushed. The caterpillar is now so different, it probably wouldn't want to have stayed the same.

I too am different, and I'm pleased to say I have not only survived but I have been told I have also enabled others to flourish and shine. Being vibrant is my goal, despite my past; I have chosen to change. The caterpillar was limited to the ground; now, transformed, it can fly with no limits.

The cover of this book is how I like to see the bright, beautiful colours in life shining as we burst through what keeps us down. The bursting through the paper signifies that the past is not as strong as we think it is – it can be broken, ripped away.

The ripple shows how we start immediately to change the vibrations we make to those around us.

I often have a sense that others are watching me, to see if I can complete what I set out to do. Will I get to the top of my mountain? There could be a tribe of women behind me, waiting to gain strength for their own lives. Could there be more, as the ripples spread further? Will I ever really know? Whether there is or not, I will hold these ladies in mind and let that help me to keep going.

You might be surprised how much of your time is taken up by comparing and competition – probably far more than you realise. It can affect our everyday and our whole-life plans. Catching those thoughts and turning them around for good could change the course of your whole life.

So what are we doing with our time? I have given this much thought.

'Is this worth doing? What is it going to achieve? Is it just a dream, a cathartic exercise, or is it going to help other people truly live a better life?'

Some of these questions are hard to answer, but they led me to look at how I was spending my time. I found I was competing with myself many hours of the day. Writing meant I wasn't counselling, organising my home life or spending time with my family and friends. Was it worth it to shut myself away to write? I stood back from this to observe how I was feeling within myself. I realised I was content when I was allowing myself to write and letting go of the guilt of not being somewhere else or doing something else. I had committed to this and was going to jolly well enjoy it!

SMG

I came up with the following little test to see whether I was doing the right things with my time:

- Sense – does it make sense? If it does, then stay with the key thing as the main focus.
- Meaning – does it create more meaning in your life? Is it creating purpose for your life, time and career?
- Gratitude – does it gain gratitude from others? Or is it gaining financial gratitude.

This checklist helped me decide to step out and move forward beyond my doubt. The fact that the initials of the words spell out my initials, SMG, help me remember it, so I hope it will stay with you too, to help you measure decisions going forward.

A couple of years ago I was thrilled to become a member of the Association of Christian Writers (ACW) and then to be asked to be a speaker at their Bath Writers' Day with writer, editor and publisher Nicki Copeland. On receiving my first copy of the quarterly magazine, I was enlightened and slightly intimidated by such great writing! I thoroughly enjoyed reading Jane Brocklehurst's article on 'Fear of Success'. I had always thought this was a hidden fear not many knew about!

Jane wrote this article in the Spring 2019 issue of the magazine, straight from her heart. She spoke about her own writing career and the challenges of comparison, as she had seen a friend achieving publication while she had not as yet been published. She looked at her friend's life and asked herself whether she would have wanted to go through such challenges in order to have those topics to write about. She decided not. She then looked at her fears to see what might get in the way of being successful.

Jane writes so well I believe she will achieve her dream of being published. However, beyond that is her willingness to look at her 'stuff'. Her openness to talk about it and see that fears are real: fear of success, of her inadequacies, of feeling out of her depth, of expectations she cannot fulfil and of letting people down. These can be confused with fear of failure, but fear of success is also something that we can hide behind.

We can get caught up in doing and repeating what we do without thinking about our motivation. The checklist above should help you see whether something you are doing or were going to add into your life is worth the time and energy. We are multi-faceted personalities who need stimulation, yet over-scheduling and planning can take away our creativity.

The competition for our time steals away the creative flare and takes away our peace and joy. When light sparkles into a diamond, the many facets reflect and refract the light. We can do that too, given the right light and space.

The many aspects of our lives and ourselves can shine, given the right nourishment to our soul. I hesitate to mention the opposite, as my heart sinks as I think of it, but sadly there are many cases of this. My thoughts go straight to a young child I counsel who has been abused by both her parents because of their addictive behaviour. She shows such trauma, as she received very little nurturing. The strain is visible in her eyes and she competes with others for love, food and attention, even though there is no need for her to do that any longer.

She can't trust that nurture and nourishment will be provided for her. She fears it will disappear any moment,

especially if she does something wrong. Yet given time in play therapy, she reveals herself as intelligent, switched on, bright, funny and loveable. She is finding herself in play as I witness this child 'be a child' again. Her pain pulls on my heartstrings. She is showing me who she really is, yet she will struggle to show the world until she is slowly healed in her heart. This is possible but needs a lot of patience from her new family as they demonstrate unconditional love and normal family life.

The Pleasure of Play

I love play therapy with children in my private practice, as it enables them to show me what is hard to put into words. So much so that I now also provide creative therapy for adults, as it enables them to do the same. Play!

When play is confused by competition and achieving, it can take away from the real purpose of play. Not being good at sport or art at school, for example, can leave us no longer playing.

Play can be seen as frivolous, just for fun and without purpose. I remember a time before my training where that fun seemed such a waste of time and it would even annoy me. I had no time for that! Then, watching children, I realised that when we lose the sense of play, we lose so much. I gained it back and now I love to play. This for me is still structured, as one of the ways I play is to dance, but I am finding my way to dancing freely. Brené Brown describes this well in her book *Daring Greatly*. This book challenged the therapist in me: after structured training it is hard to let go again.

However, I cannot emphasise enough how freeing it has been to allow myself to play and dance freely again. Time spent without purpose is time well spent to free our minds and bodies.

When we play, we can express what is stuck or needs expressing from our subconscious mind. Children show me what is going on in this play and being able to mirror this back to them to help them make sense is wonderful. There are many aspects to play that we can openly learn from.

Playing with ideas is one way of discovering our calling. One client talked of horses with such passion, and I helped her find a new purpose in life using them in therapy.

Finding and staying true to our calling and not getting distracted by others' journeys is key to fully living. We can get stuck by jealousy and resentment. I have total admiration for those around me who have stayed true to their path.

Failing Intelligently

One such person is the author Caris Grimes whose book, *Failing Intelligently*, I have been privileged to publish.

Very often, the topic of a manuscript when it first lands in my inbox is a key point of decision for me. To be honest, I was nervous and yet intrigued with the topic of failure. It appealed to my role as a psychotherapist within the publishing field. Also, it grabbed my attention because Caris is a surgeon.
Malcolm was happy to say to me,
'Here is one for you!'

I like to meet and talk with an author to get a sense of them. This will give me an idea of how we will work together. Quite often the theme of a manuscript will come out somewhere during the process, so you can see why I was a little nervous. Would this book come about, or would it fail to make it through the many hurdles in the publishing process?

As the theme of a manuscript can play out as the book evolves, I really wondered how this was going to go.

Would it fail and, if so, would that be intelligently or epically?!

Even to the last moment, on the day of the book launch, we were waiting for the books to arrive, otherwise I would be holding the one and only copy available to us.

My thoughts were, 'Is this the moment of failure?'

Would my fear of failing Caris take over? I had to be mindful of this.

Fear of failure can be worse than failure itself; it can be paralysing and stop us acting at all. Thankfully, Caris has, with the help of her faith, conquered this too. She was not watching what others were doing or saying but staying with the belief that this book needed to be written and published. There was no room for failure – she had worked through her own fear in order to get the book out there. No room for comparison and competition: just the destination of this book arriving.

All the books under Malcolm Down and Sarah Grace Publishing are 'dyslexia friendly'. I am dyslexic, so Caris's book is fitting, as fear of failure is a daily battle for me and others with dyslexia.

Often it feels like we can be tripped up at any hurdle. We may be able to tackle a task one day yet the next day that same task is difficult.

However, knowing it is there and working with the effects, by being honest with ourselves and others of how it may play out and affect them, helps everyone manage better. This is not an excuse but rather an informed understanding of our limitations and strengths: owning them and recognising them helps. On difficult days I try not to compare myself to my better days, but go with what is happening that day. So if I am struggling with numbers, I will leave my accounts that day if I can, and wait for it to pass. I might find spelling difficult one day so I will delay writing that email until I am less tired and see if it comes more easily.

I guess I have learnt not to sweat the small stuff and to see the bigger picture of life. Live and let live comes to mind here, as competition with ourselves and others can make life incredibly blurred. Is it thoughts in our head or is there really a competition going on? Making sense of this and letting go of the mental battle can be such a relief and so rewarding, as it is exhausting to keep a mental battle going on with no resolve.

It's important to recognise the conversation in our mind, to capture the thoughts by speaking them out, perhaps to a counsellor, to make sense of them. It can be hugely valuable to make ourselves this vulnerable, and as we move away from it we recognise how damaging it would have been to stay there.

So having received Caris's manuscript, my first task was to read it, and then to meet the author. So I met Caris, and what a delight! Malcolm and I found every step of the way with her book to be very relaxed, uplifting and enjoyable.

I have learnt from Caris, as I do with every author. She has enlightened me and encouraged me probably without even knowing it. I feel her book will do the same for many people.

It is a book to pick up time and time again in times of struggles or just to refresh us. One of the endorsements for in the book says,

    'A kind, gentle and refreshingly honest walk through every aspect of failure that left me feeling relieved and encouraged.'

I thank Caris for taking the plunge, for embracing the journey of failing, learning from it and rising above it. The opposite is less appealing – it's not so pretty, not so refreshing; it's self-destructive and we get stuck. Caris demonstrates how to see it differently by making ourselves vulnerable, as she embarked on a long journey of writing a book on failure from many angles.

I am in awe of every author, no matter what the topic is, and I feel privileged to have been on this journey with Caris. I am thankful for that task she gave me and I am thrilled with the cover. I am also delighted that she has a great team around her to help market the book. I would say she has embraced failing beyond measure.

In her book, Caris has made it easier to digest a difficult topic. The book is small enough to handle yet the content is big enough to make a difference in people's lives, including my own.

The ripple effect from failure is easy to see and often difficult to make sense of. Yet one positive consequence of owning our part in failing and of forgiving is that we can change many lives too. Let's start to look at our own – let the ripple be positive and flow in the right direction.

So let's start to appreciate each other more. As women especially I believe we can collaborate to bring about more. Caris uses her experiences of break-up and surgical failures to inform her writing. Behind each woman who has done well, I would like to bet that, as for me, there is a past that could have taken her down. If we use our experience and turn it round for good, it can be what drives us in a healthy way. It's not the failing that we need to look at now; it's the getting up, and if you have fallen, you have that choice too.

Find friends who want to see you get up again and who will celebrate your results with you. Find the right place to be so that you can be encouraged and allowed to shine again. If you are that friend, then I applaud you, especially if the women you are supporting are reaching the heights you would like to climb but you are not there yet.

On the other hand, if you are a friend who cannot see another achieve without quietly hoping they fall, may I encourage you to listen to that small voice. Speak this out with someone to help find the root of the pain it has come from.

Counselling again is ideal, but otherwise seek someone with whom you feel comfortable to be that vulnerable. It may well have a root back in your childhood, perhaps of sibling rivalry or a past hurt, or maybe your home life now is not all you would like it to be. Whatever the cause, you can live free of it, and help yourself and your friends to move on together.

Background Noise

What is in the background for you? What are the noises, the voices that stop you moving forward? Mine can sound like this:

- Can you keep up? (This comes from trying to measure up to older brothers, like pedalling like mad to keep up on my bike!)
- Can you stay in control?
- You will fail . . .

While travelling in the USA, I enjoy visiting different types of churches. One such place in Richmond, Virginia, was Richmond Community Church. My friend and I were so warmly welcomed and were even given a goodie bag! In this bag was a little book, *5 Habits of Happy People*. This church leader was speaking my language!

One habit mentioned in this book was avoiding comparisons. This statement stood out: 'Avoid the "highlight reelism".'

We often tend to compare others' highs against our average or weak points. We play in our mind the film of perfection, watching the good things others are doing or have done. We need to reel that film back in and play a new one for ourselves, one that plays our own achievements and better days so that we are keeping ourselves grounded and centred. Remembering that this is not necessary based in reality but rather it is the perception in our minds will help stop that film.

Gracelets

Let's truly celebrate who we are and our gifts – not competing but being able to walk alongside others and encourage them to be the best they can be.

What better gift is there than really feeling alive and being able to encourage someone else to feel the same.

If we are more outward looking, does that help our own lives heal and stay fulfilled? On my Christian journey I see this frequently – there are good results all round as long as we do it from a good heart.

Something I wrote down years ago that God spoke to me recently touched my heart again, so I will share it with you:
   'My plan for you is for the fullness of who I am to be revealed in the fullness of who you are.'

How huge is that?! It blows my mind. To keep checking in to see if it is happening is rather cool. I cannot make it happen, but I keep listening each day. If I am feeling jealous of someone, I need to check why – is there something I should be doing or have to be aware of about my calling? It is good for us to see what comes up for us when we are challenged. It may be difficult; it may hurt, but if we can grow from it and stay true to ourselves and our calling then it is worth the examination of ourselves.

As we embrace our own calling, we become the best we can be, rather than looking to another to validate us. We can then help others to recognise their strengths. We do not need to take from others, to sell their ideas as our own. Ideally, we should feel confident that others have our best interests at heart.

All this should enhance our own lives and the lives of others, as we live in the way God intended us to. Can we consider standing side by side, interlinking to bring more of God's Kingdom?

One person, Nicki Copeland, allowed me to see how this is possible. We met and shared our ideas before speaking at the ACW Writers' Day together. What a blessing, and it went so well! Collaboration at its best. I knew we would work together again and I had the privilege of asking her to edit this book.

We do not know where it may lead when we take small steps of sharing, not fearfully protecting our own bit, but rather working together for the good of others.

Blessed to be a blessing – what a way to live.

Dancing freely in the Spirit is one of the newest areas of freedom I have experienced. I stepped out to engage in this at the gathering in Ireland I mentioned earlier. A lovely lady called Anna complimented the way I danced. She had no idea that was the first moment of just stepping out and enjoying the Irish music with no fear of others. It encouraged me no end, yet she did not need to encourage me, so I give thanks for her and for that moment. I hope this will help you step out to encourage someone, even if you think they don't need it. We have no idea of the good it might do.

Your Ripple

What comparison holds you back or draws you away from what you have been created to do?

Knowingly or not, in many cases we compare ourselves to our siblings. Is this the case for you?

Is it time to look and see how this has helped or hindered your path in life?

Consider these values:

- ▸ Does it make sense?
- ▸ Does it bring meaning?
- ▸ Does it bring gratitude to you or others?

Is there anything that needs looking at in your life that is not bringing these values?

What does the noise in the background sound like for you, the voice that repeats and catches you out?

Do you find you can play freely or does it turn to competition and become about achievement?

Would you like to add more play into your life?

Can you share this with others and address its effect on you? Please don't forget you are not doing this alone.

Chapter 6

Boarded Heart

As we continue on our journey of unpacking, we are now at the heart of the book, so it is time to examine our hearts in more detail. We need to look at our heart health. This is often a topic of conversation I hear talked about within Christian circles with regard to our emotional health. However, I find more widely that heart health is generally only on the radar if someone has a medical issue.

As mentioned previously, I had the privilege of working with Mark Stibbe on his book *Home at Last*. This book is very helpful both for adults who went to boarding school and for their families, and it has had a big impact on many lives.

Sent away to boarding school on his eighth birthday, Mark Stibbe watched his adoptive parents drive down a gravel road. Mark was left standing in front of a huge country house with his trunk and his teddy. That night, already confused and frightened, he was given the first beating at his new home.

In this ground-breaking book, Mark contends that there are many wounded people just like him, men and women who suffer throughout their lives with homesick souls. This often leads to being driven to succeed at work yet failing to connect emotionally.

Boarding our hearts can be done unconsciously, without awareness of when it started to happen. This term I use, 'boarded heart', has come from my work with certain clients: ex-boarders, those who were sent away at an early age to boarding school. Originally a gift to privileged English children, boarding-school education has rippled out across the world over time.

As we have already looked at early childhood issues, you will know where I am going with this.

Children sent away 'for the making of them', for their 'own good', would have to push down many emotions to be respectful and to protect themselves and their parents. It can create a huge dilemma:

'How can I complain, as this is a privilege, yet I'm in agony here. But they have paid for it and it is the best thing for me.'

Yet the pain is so deep. I have heard of many stories of the sheer agony of separation from family, friends, pets and home – from all that is familiar. Yet to cry would be dangerous, as others would not cope with their tears; vulnerability feels dangerous. Many parents can't bear the separation either, so they put on a brave face. Maybe it would surface their own emotions, from their own experience, so the pain gets pushed down. Abandonment, loss, abuse or the threat of abuse, loss of freedom: all create a shutting-down of emotions to survive.

I will not go too much into the school system or the theory of detachment and trauma, as I will mention some good books that cover this in the further-reading section. For now, it is important to understand what happens when we shut down, and to be aware of the cycle of pain.

The boarded heart defence is absolutely brilliant in terms of survival skills. But it comes at great cost. I realise now that my own boarded heart sadly stopped me feeling and believing anything real. I watched my brothers doing things and hid away. I would jump out and have a go, then dive back in. And when I cried I couldn't stop, and I would be told that was enough.

Why did no one ask me why I was crying in the first place?

Why did no one hold me till I stopped hurting?

I can only assume they couldn't bear my pain, as maybe they had never managed to experience their own.

In a Nutshell

Being repeatedly sent away from loved ones has to be endured by boarders, and often crying is not acceptable or encouraged. You may have seen the episode of *The Crown* on Netflix where Prince Philip is sent away to boarding school, as Prince Charles would be later on. This gives us a good idea of what it would be like; even for those who are not of royal descent, there is an expectation that they will cope.

Another good film which you can find on YouTube is *The Making of Them*, based on the book by Nick Duffell.[5] There is a scene that makes my heart ache, where a young boy speaks of school in an adult way as he adjusts his heart to cope. Then, when he is asked about home, he is suddenly a true young boy.

---

[5] Nick Duffle, *The Making of Them* (Lone Arrow Press, 2000).

He has not completely disassociated (cut off his emotions) but is splitting, (taking on two ways of being), to cope with being in an institution that is not home. Emotions are cut off, and matter-of-fact thinking has to happen. Conforming and pleasing adults and superiors has to be learnt.

Those under stress find it difficult to cope emotionally; they might freeze completely, shut down and walk away, become aggressive, or demonstrate no reaction at all and have no memory of the incident. Many emotions could be happening but the processing of these emotions is hard to control. There can be a huge fear of letting any emotion out for fear of its power. Not knowing what we may or may not be capable of is very hard to manage.

Many will rebel and over time they may even become abusers to avoid being abused. This is a way of regaining the control. There are many levels of shame to cope with, or perhaps to bury.

Even a good experience of school may leave its mark, such as a residue of detached decisions, unable to make decisions and lack of compassion for others at times. We are not designed to live in an institution but a caring family, so there will always be effects.

Many of our leaders and politicians went to boarding school as children. My heart aches for them, for us and for the way the British Empire led the way with regard to sending children away.

We must also consider missionaries to other countries, many of whose children were also put into schools and homes. It was all done for good, but the pain is the same. Many missionary schools were a mixed blessing too.

Children left in orphanages also experience that loss and pain. No matter the reason for being left, the pain is the same.

Going back to boarding schools, one link that has often come up in my work with clients, to my surprise, is that in many schools the academic work did not seem to be particularly important. Parents were paying, and as long as they paid and the children turned up it was a good arrangement.

I found this remarkable: was this not meant to be the 'making of them'?

Or was it more of a childminding service?

Was the 'making of them' simply to make them tough and strong? That doesn't seem to work too well either, as many who come into my counselling room are struggling. The motivation to do well in sport seems strong, as this gets you noticed. Creative children nearly always appear to struggle in such an environment.

Breaking the Shell

One day, my lovely friends Andy and Lindsay handed me some freshly harvested walnuts. I cracked them open one by one. I was just about to eat one when I looked into it. It had cracked right through the middle.

The walnut is covered by a hard shell to protect it from the world. The inside is fruitful, delicious, healthy and good to eat. The white part is the soft, fleshy part. As I looked at it, I considered how it looked like a heart healing, where the darker areas are those still in need of healing.

I used this image with a client, as mentioned in the following story:

What? Me Have Counselling?!

This was my outlook until very recently. I had always dismissed counselling as something other, weaker people needed. It was most definitely something I didn't need, and there was no way I was going to submit to that!

I had struggled with self-confidence since early childhood. I sometimes had a short fuse and I knew my marriage was suffering, yet I told myself I was OK. I could handle it; I could change my poor communication and deal with the lows that life had flung my way.

That was how I was brought up: don't show emotion; just bottle it up and move on. The trouble was, that scheme didn't work, and rather than face up to it at the explosive points, I would walk away from the situation and hide in my shell.

At the age of seven I was sent to a weekly boarding school. Until I went for counselling, I had thought I was OK. At thirteen I went to a public school as a boarder, which meant I rarely saw my parents or my sister. I missed out on a huge chunk of family life.

I can remember my first day at boarding school very vividly: I had a feeling of being totally abandoned and alone. On the first evening I was on the receiving end of some verbal bullying, which destroyed any confidence I had and set the tone for my next five years of school life.

It produced a fear that any time I walked into a room where there was a group of people, I believed they were all talking about me and putting me down. If I responded badly to something or made a wrong comment to someone, I believed they would use it against me.

My wife gave me *Home at Last*, about boarding school trauma, and I read it reluctantly! I then read it again alongside a friend who was having difficulties and asked me to help, and slowly I began to realise I needed help too.

And after a particularly stormy moment in my marriage, my wife just said,
'It's down to you. There's a counsellor mentioned at the end of the book. Why don't you contact her?'

In other words, she was close to having had enough; the situation was destroying us both. So I contacted the counsellor.

Over a period of months my skilful counsellor prised open my hard shell and I began to realise that the causes of my behaviour were rooted deep in the past. She showed me a walnut in its shell, and said,
'I wonder if this resonates with you?'

Silence followed, as it was almost beyond words. I had just seen, for the first time ever, how I had been feeling. I had a layer of protection around my heart, just like the shell. As the shell was opened, these feelings were revealed, then the way to healing became clear. Now I'm believing who I am in the eyes of God – loved and valued.

I have asked for prayer many times on this journey! And my life has changed. I am happy with who I am and am working at recognising some behavioural triggers before retreating into my shell.

In all this, I have come to see and realise that many of us are affected and messed up by being abandoned – not just those who have been hurt by the boarding school effect. It can range from being left in an orphanage, being fostered, latchkey children, lack of parental support and affirmation, divorce (both their own and parental divorce), redundancy, bereavement, suffering abuse, to mention just a few. But there is hope! Jesus knows what being abandoned is like and longs to heal us. God can put 'Humpty Dumpty' back together, even better than before. Once I thought,

'Why don't I get asked to help and join in?'

Now, I'm being asked if I can take things on and help bring healing and significance to others.

Here is another client's story after reading *Home at Last*:

Sally's story

At twenty-one I met and fell in love with the man who was to be my husband.

He had grown up in a very dysfunctional Italian family, and when he was seven his parents decided to emigrate to England and place him in a strict home, where he was to remain with no personal contact with his parents for four years.

We married and had two delightful children, but I couldn't ignore the emotional gulf between myself and my husband; we remained distant. Periodically I would raise the subject, only to meet a wall of denial, and I was often accused of imagining stuff. Was this a cultural thing? I could not work him out and felt isolated within a marriage that had lacked intimacy, shared joys and laughter. He had no confidence and started to have panic attacks, which he always reasoned away. I made allowances for his behaviour and gradually became a facilitator. He was very safety conscious, never initiated anything and absolutely refused to talk about feelings – mine or his.

At the age of fifty I finally admitted to myself that I was in the same cage as him. Throughout our marriage there had been numerous opportunities for him to get help, with little impact on our lives. It must have consumed lots of energy to keep up appearances, using denial and blame to hold himself together. Every once in a while I went public with friends about the difficulties, nobody seemed to get it, and I might just as well have imagined everything. Self-doubt heaped up; maybe this was all I should expect in a marriage.

Things changed dramatically when I read a book on Boarding School Syndrome that a friend recommended to my husband; it was just the right time. A few pages in, I felt utterly vindicated, a revelation that filled me with joy and hope. He was able to meet with that friend and work through the book and I was able to see a counsellor, which he would do later.

That was over a year and a half ago and I have found it immensely worthwhile. It is the beginning of a new season.

I have been able to change the way I see the man I love who had brought his fear and pain into our marriage and was so boarded up he created a whole new person to hide behind (his words, not mine).

My hope is that one day our precious marriage of nearly five decades will see much more laughter and fun shared, along with feelings! Our children have already seen the ripple effect!

How wonderful to hear about the changes in these people's lives and the ripples out to their families and friends.

Paving the Way

As I have previously mentioned, the pioneering voice in this area is Nick Duffell, whose books *The Making of Them* and *Wounded Leaders* paved the way for Mark Stibbe to write *Home at Last*. I studied Nick's books during my counselling training, as I had been in a process group at university with an ex-boarder and I saw how it had affected him. During my placement year, I worked with a charity called The Living Room, working with addicts.

My first two clients, one male and the other female, had both been to boarding school, and I started to see links in behaviour. Strangely, I was able to relate to them, even though I had not been to boarding school myself. I assumed this was because I had developed similar coping strategies, having boarded my heart to protect it from pain. I will tell you more about this later.

When Mark Stibbe came to our publishing house with his manuscript, I was initially reluctant to work with him. Mark was unfortunately pressing a number of my buttons that touched my own wounded heart.

There were many familiarities with his story and my ex-husband's – more than just sharing a name! I had to really work hard to work through my own pain to even attend our *Home at Last* meetings. There were about fifteen of us supporting Mark and Cherith, praying and eating together as we created a team to work with those who had suffered as a result of going to boarding school.

Yet, working through this process, I realised how much work I had already done in that area. It was one of those moments where I found myself saying,
    'That's what all this has been about!'

Little did I know I would start working with so many ex-boarders and their families, as we decided to put the details of my counselling service in the back of Mark's book.

As we worked on the book with Mark, I kept a very close eye on the content. I even held it up at the last moment, risking it not being ready for the launch, as I felt we needed to clarify something for the reader. It was published on the day of the EU referendum and the first print run sold out within a month!

This has led me to find a counselling supervisor who knows this subject well, so now I am supervised by Joy Schaverien, who was the first to write on boarding school syndrome. I am privileged to have her supporting me and I really feel I am in the right place. As you read further in this chapter about my links with boarding school, you will also see how relevant it is that I work with Joy.

It is interesting to unpack the trunk for ex-boarders. So many have had to put their belongings away into their trunk along with their heart, their feelings, their reliance on another at a young age. To take that all out of the trunk at once would be too much, as a huge fear of being 'undone' can rise up. I reassure them that we are doing it together and there is no rush.

Perhaps this is a bit like renovating a building: it has to be done in the right order and it takes time. I hope, as we work together, it will not feel like being undone but rather coming home at last.

A Big Jigsaw Piece

I have recently discovered, at a meeting with my cousins, that my birth father went to boarding school! It felt as though a big jigsaw piece dropped into place. I felt that meeting him put the last piece into place, yet I still had so much to learn from him and the ripple he left behind.

Once I re-established contact with him as an adult, my dad was only in my life for two short years. During that time we got on well, yet there was a distance that was hard to bridge. I thought it was because I had not grown up with him, but I am convinced now that it was a result of his lack of attachment to his own parents. This would have made it hard for him to form deep attachments to us, his children. I felt that it was a pull-and-push kind of relationship. I would move closer emotionally, yet he wasn't there. He made some moves towards me, which I then found hard to respond to.

With the benefit of hindsight, I realise that I found his tentative moves towards me hard to receive for fear he would disappear again; maybe his fear was the same.

One painful conversation damaged us both. He revealed to me,

'You know, it was incredibly hard leaving you and your brother, so much so I had a breakdown.'

I was shocked and stared at him as I had had no knowledge of this and wondered why my mum had never told me.

'Dad, I didn't know that.'

'Yes, and your mother did not come and see me once.'

I visualised her looking after me, as a sick baby, and my brother who was eighteen months old and not yet walking. Additionally, she was sick with undiagnosed diabetes. Dad had left for another woman, leaving Mum to look after us. My mum and I were in and out of hospital, creating further separation issues for me and my brother. Yet my dad was only concerned about his own care. This hurt me and shocked me all at once. I wanted to shout at him,

'Did you come back now to tell me you loved me, or did you come to tell me how angry you were at not being cared for?'

Finding out that he had been to boarding school after being evacuated at the age of five, instead of being in his own home with his parents and sister, I started to make sense of things. Clearly, he was still trying to resolve the very deep pain of not being taken care of and of feeling abandoned. Soon after we had met for the first time, he shared that he was afraid I would not want to continue a relationship with him. The fear of abandonment was still incredibly strong.

This did cross my mind when I was being brave and seeking to find him:

'What if he doesn't want to know me?'

'What if he has died already?'

'What if we are just too different?'

Many fears rose up, but I pushed them away as I needed to know who he was and find out more about him. The final jigsaw-puzzle piece now helped me to make more sense of 'me': where my creativity came from, my fine blonde hair, my small stature and my sensitive nature. He was all these things and more.

Having met my dad ten years ago, to find out recently that he went to boarding school has been a revelation. For the last nine years I have been studying, working with and getting involved with conferences for ex-boarders. How amazing is that? I instinctively knew that this was a group of people I connected with but wasn't sure why. I had tried to make sense of it – my father was an evacuee; I had learnt to disassociate to cope with my own family life – yet to find that I was a daughter of an ex-boarder went a long way to explaining why the attachment had been missing totally from a very young age. He could not make the emotional connections he needed to make in order to be there for me, and this played out through not being there as a father.

My brother emigrated to Australia; it isn't unusual for ex-boarders and their children to be far apart.

I see it as a safe distance as well as an unconscious act by the child – 'I will abandon you now' – having been sent away to boarding school or not having been parented well.When I met my dad for the first time I was intrigued, scared, excited and nervous – these were just a few of the emotions I could even start to describe! I can remember all the moments just before, like it was happening in slow motion. Getting to the pub and getting out of the car, walking in and then seeing him. Hugging and crying. Talking for hours. Seeing photos of family members I had never met yet had known existed . . . it all felt surreal.

Letting go . . .

A few meetings in, I was feeling frustrated at how different my life could have been if my dad had not walked out and then showed very little care by not even staying in touch. I wanted to say to him,

'What were you thinking, just to walk away and not check we were OK?'

I was feeling that everything I had endured with my five stepbrothers and my stepfather was my dad's fault because he hadn't been there to protect me. Yet I wanted this relationship to develop and I knew he couldn't handle hearing all that. So I looked at this old man and thought,

'We have the now, and we can move on from here.'

I made a decision to leave the anger and the frustration behind at that point and to continue to get to know this man, my dad, and was able to start to feel love for him. What a journey!

Kintsugi or Cracked Pots

I love to hear about new subjects from different sources. I get excited to hear about something that starts a ripple and changes many lives. This time it was Kintsugi, an idea from a Japanese art form that has moved around our world to touch many.

Kintsugi is golden joinery, where the artist makes something broken into something more beautiful. The method dates back to the fifteenth century, using resin to repair the pot, then covering it with gold. The gold transforms the pot into a new and beautiful creation, of much more worth and value than it was before. Nothing is wasted; nothing is thrown away, but it is added to because it already had worth.

As I researched Kintsugi, I came across Patrick Regan who wrote *Honesty Over Silence* with Lisa Hoeksma[6] and started a charity called Kintsugi Hope. His book is great for everyone, but especially for men, along with its journal *This Is Me*. Soon after this, a client brought the book to show me, and then a while after that Patrick was speaking at a conference I attended.

It was a real pleasure to hear him speak my language of opening up conversations and enabling healing. His charity helps many people, offering hope and changing the ripple in a huge way over time. I thank the Lord for you, Patrick!

Through my faith in God I see that he has added gold into my life. I am still here, although I could have died many times owing to ill health, abuse, accidents and a bomb.

---

[6] Patrick Regan and Liza Hoeksma, *Honesty Over Silence* (CWR, 2018).

Broken Pots.

Behind the Garden House Hospice there's a little wooden shed where I go to sit when I feel the need for a moment of a quiet reflection. Around the door of the shed there is a collection of old earthenware pots, all shapes and sizes, and all with their own unique characteristics and little imperfections, just like us. At my feet lies a little broken pot that has been cast aside, too badly broken to be of any use. Sitting here with the little broken pot growing warm in my hands, I think of all the broken people who have held my hand and asked me why? Why has this happened to me? I don't know why, no-one knows why. But the little broken pot in my hands seems to tell me, in its own silent way, that we are all broken, one way or another. And that in some mysterious way this brokenness somehow makes us even more human, in our vulnerability and need for care and compassion.

When my moment of quiet reflection is over, I carry the little broken pot back into the hospice with me and place it on the window of our quiet room, where people come to find some sense of peace among all their brokenness. Before I go off duty, I look in on my little pot, now bathed in moonlight casting silvery blue shadows on the window. I notice that someone has lit a little candle and placed it beside my broken pot. Perhaps the little pot has spoken, in its own silent way, to someone else's heart. The candle seems to highlight all the little pots imperfections, casting deep shadows among all the broken bits. But when I put the candle inside the little pot, its inner beauty is revealed as the light streams out through every crack and crevice, transforming it into a work of art? Or a symbol of light shining in the darkness? Or perhaps even a symbol of inner healing. Because the little pot doesn't look broken any more, and its fragility only seems to deepen its sense of translucent beauty.

The thing about symbols is that they can speak to us in a way that transcends words. Sitting here in the moonlight with the little broken pot glowing warmly in my hands, it speaks to me once again, in its own silent way. It tells me that we don't have to be afraid of being broken, or try to hide it by pretending to be perfect, because no-one is perfect. And that its through our brokenness that we become more sensitive to the brokenness of others and more open to give and to receive care and compassion. It is then that our hidden human beauty is most truly revealed, precisely through our fragility and brokenness.

The little broken pot now lives permanently on the window of the hospice quiet room with a little light burning day and night inside it. It still speaks to many people in its own silent way. I sometimes wonder if the little broken pot and I were destined to meet, like soul mates. There is an American Indian prayer which asks God for the wisdom to understand the secret which he has hidden under every leaf and rock. The secret which I found hidden in the little broken pot is that there is an eternal beauty hidden within every human soul that can sometimes only be seen when we are at our most vulnerable and fragile. It is then that the light shines out through all our brokenness to make us whole again.

Doug Murray ©

I am still here for a reason, and he keeps adding more gold each time I am up against another difficult part of my journey. I do not always remember this, though, and may panic and board my heart again. However, given time to calm down and centre on God, I find my way back again – with added sparkle, I hope! Now if that does not give us hope in ourselves, then I am not sure what will! I believe change can happen, that healing can be a positive thing to bring about a more beautiful life, a more whole 'you'.

Even at the end of a life this is true. I have seen someone dying peacefully as they have made sense of their brokenness. My friend Paul showed me that this was possible when our goal was to get him into a wheelchair and to the chapel of the hospice. He showed me a poem about a broken pot that Doug Murrey, who worked as a senior staff nurse at the hospice, had written. Paul told me he had found peace.[7]

Finding this piece once again, I emailed the hospice to see if Doug was happy for me to use it. Two years had passed since I shared it with Paul in the hospice, so it was a long shot. How wonderful to hear back with permission to use it, and that he remembered Paul as well. It was a warming feeling to know it had encouraged Paul, and the ripple went back to Doug, to know it was still making a difference.

Too Broken?

A friend of mine recently said,
    'I am too broken and cannot be in a relationship.'

---

[7] Doug Murrey, 'Broken Pots', used with permission.

This came as a surprise to me, as I saw a beautiful, intelligent, precious lady before me with so much compassion and love in her heart for others. Why should damage from a previous relationship leave her there.

No! I wasn't having this! So I said to her,
    'Really, I don't think the damage you're feeling now will be forever. You feel hurt, and it's raw right now. I don't believe God wants you to stay in a hurt place. We can learn from each experience and you can grow from this.'

We explored the relationship that had ended, which had been emotionally abusive for her. She had lost her confidence and felt she had nothing to give. I decided that each day I would send her a positive message reminding her of the true authentic value and gifts I saw in her, to encourage her back to loving herself and to a place of stability.

The Boarder's Story

When we board our heart, it is difficult to be in a relationship. Issues may come around and around again with our partner. This comes from a level of trust in ourselves and in others from that very vulnerable place in our heart. It can be hard for a boarder to fully commit, to fully give of themselves.

We can remain with a boarded heart against the hurt until it can work itself out as anxiety or detachment from the ones we love. Here is a story to reflect on.

A Boarder's Reflection

When I finally opened my Pandora's box it contained a double whammy: that of being a third culture kid[8] as well as a young boarding school kid. I had travelled from Uganda to school in Kenya, then later to the UK.

It all started the term I turned seven. My parents dropped me off with my older sister, who was already a boarder. That deep memory of running, screaming, after my parents as they walked back to their car as the reality suddenly hit me. Abandoned. No going back.

My mother's first letter to me, commenting on how sad she had been that I'd been so upset, resulted in my determining that I would never let her see that again as I didn't want her to be sad. My heart was beginning to board up, I guess.

UK boarding was less oppressive and I made the most of the available opportunities. I threw myself into sport, drama, music – anything that made me feel good. I continued to build my protective armour and learnt how to keep my head down; the African girl in me knew how to make a plan, to survive. That rhythm of school term, then home, then school: I didn't know any other sort of life. At least I saw my parents every holiday.

When I was in my mid-thirties, someone said to me that 'goodbyes need looking at', which stopped me in my tracks.

---

[8] Third culture kids are those who grow up in a different culture from their parents, or a different culture from that which is on their passport. This means they are often exposed to a number of different cultural influences during their formative years.

Somewhere inside me something resonated: all was not quite well. I went for a session of prayer counselling and retrieved a few memories, then thought naively that all would now be well, before slipping into years of juggling family and work and also moving around quite a bit.

On retirement, my life suddenly hit a void: everything that had been propping me up vanished. I hit a brick wall. That person I thought I was had gone. My third-culture-kid survival techniques of assess and blend didn't work; my boarding school armour was suddenly just a shell. I'd run out of steam. I was finally forced to look inside, and all I could find were large patches of unhappiness, anger or emotionless empty spaces.

My automatic 'make a plan' kicked in. I came across *Home at Last*, the book by Mark Stibbe about the effects boarding school can have on children. As I read it, I realised it described me; there were things that had me tied up and were holding me to ransom. All I knew was that I wanted to be sorted. So I contacted the counsellor at the back of the book, Sarah Grace, and with her help, support and guidance, I found the courage to look deeply into myself.

I operate well through images and pictures and my mind brought me all sorts of illustrations to describe what I couldn't say easily with words. Slowly, with Sarah's listening and prompting, I started to look at and understand who I am and how I got here.
Bits of me were still stuck at being a seven-year-old. Gradually I made peace with myself and anyone else I found I needed to.

I started to recognise that those experiences have been a part of making me who I am today, and that's OK.
There was much to acknowledge and much to forgive.
Doing it with someone to guide me seemed to validate it, and it helped me to work out how to manage this self I was discovering.

Now I am better acquainted with and kinder to myself, so as the occasional new thing creeps out of the box, I at least feel equipped to face it, capture it and make my peace with it.

This client found a way to express herself through images and pictures. I sometimes find it helps me to do this with words.
I play with the words 'partner' and 'parent', as these can be the people closest to us, the ones we desperately want to be close to.

Partner to Parent

Here I make a link:

Partner and parent – how close these words are. Both are relationships where one is reliant on another. Parents should be able to rely on each other, as the child relies on the parents. This relationship is not meant to be broken, as that damages both the couple and the child.

- ▶ Part-ner – 'part' of another 'ner' – a pair relying on and being a part of one another.
- ▶ Par-ent – 'par' a pair make an infant who 'ent'ers the world.

Both relationships mean we have to trust and rely on another to be able to be intimate, bearing our own vulnerability and that of another person. Then both can withstand the fragility of life and the vulnerability of the child.

It is totally irrational for children to see being sent away to boarding school as their fault, that they had done something wrong, but somehow that often happens. Children do this to protect the adults in their lives. Children need adults to survive, so the shame and guilt that is felt, which is often not talked about, is taken on by the child. It is then held there, is not spoken about and then taunts them throughout life, a subconscious gagging. Getting these out in the open with a safe adult, friend or counsellor is essential for healthy lives and relationships.

This is how I survived within my home and having started working closely with boarding school survivors I can relate to this defence, even though I did not go away to school. I wished to be taken away by my real father who was going to come and save me, sweep in and take me off in his arms, knowing my pain without me even saying a word. I told my mum one day that he was coming, and she told me to stop dreaming. Now I know that that dream kept me alive on the inside.

When I heard the song 'Tomorrow' from the musical *Annie* it struck a chord so deep I realised that I had kept myself going by thinking,
    'It's OK, because when I turn six, then it will be all good';
    'When I reach such a height then I will be OK';
    'When I get to . . .' the next thing coming, just like 'Tomorrow', I would be saved. 'It will be alright when . . .'

The story continues

I am thankful to my counsellor for holding the pain I had endured within. Now I live more freely and fully. The scars are there, and I can feel pain returning sometimes when I feel controlled by another. I am more able to see why and where it is coming from. If I overreact to something I am more able to go back and rationalise it, to make sense of it having addressed it. I try not to let things simmer and stay under the surface but bring them into conversation.

The hardest time is when others do not want to address things and there is a sense of secret, unspoken issues. This will bring about a sense of dread, as insecure thoughts and feelings come up. The unknown that I grew up in is revisited, yet it does not have the sting that it did. I can sense it easily, which can be a good thing, as it can be addressed and then the same pattern can be avoided.

Especially Femininity

Another area that is given little attention in boarding up our hearts is femininity. I have counselled many women who were not celebrating their womanhood, their female bodies and their beauty.

I noticed that one client, who had been to boarding school, started to mimic me as if she were watching what I wore, how I wore it and how I did my hair. As we were talking, she started to hold her hair up like the way mine was styled. It was an unconscious act, I could tell, as she was trying to identify with me.

This made me realise that my own journey had not been straightforward in this area either, and I had had to learn this too.

Growing up surrounded by boys and teased for the slightest of differences, I squashed down my female traits, my longing to be feminine. It brought too much attention and went from embarrassment to humiliation very quickly. I learnt to not show my femininity, express it or enjoy it. I then went into agriculture as a career, which compounded it. Hunter wellies and Barbour coats were not so flattering and I was determined not to be labelled as one of the 'Nail Varnish Brigade'!

During my training I learnt to see that my classically dressed mum had managed to hold on to her own femininity. She had dressed smartly, in classic and ladylike styles and she made sure I did too, if I wasn't in wellies. But now it was a time for me to enjoy more: more colour, more of my own style, more variety and more femininity, without listening to anyone's voice but my own. Bit by bit the smart was infused with pretty and more playful. I now love clothes, flowers in my hair and especially summer clothes with lots of colour. I can wear black; I can wear anything I like! I now get compliments, which I would not have done before, as I was hiding, just like the boarding school ladies I was seeing. I ached to see them blossom and flourish in colour and style too.

Gracelets

We are designed to fully live, to live in full colour not in black and white.

If we decide to stay in the brokenness and to block out the golden shimmers, are we not staying as cracked pots?

At desperate times it might seem easier to remain there; it can be hard to pull ourselves out.

So, let's see what is blocking our heart, what have we boarded against, what we are blocking out.

As mentioned, we often fear what we could be capable of. Often our anger is behind this, and it can feel terrifying.

What would happen if I were to let go and all that anger were to come out?

Is it best buried and left to die inside?

Sadly, we start to die inside if we leave it there. Stewing on our own juices and always fearful: what a sad place to be.

We are most often more fearful of what we are capable of than what we are not capable of. Hidden anger can be most scary and is to be avoided at all costs.

A Good Recipe
If we can take time to hear – to listen and be with ourselves and with God – it is remarkable what can happen.

My recipe:

- ▶ Take some time away from the world.
- ▶ Be with yourself.
- ▶ Then take the letter 'T' from the word 'TIME'.
- ▶ This leaves I ME – let yourself be you with your own thoughts, not others' voices in your mind, but your own.
- ▶ This leaves us in a place to HEAR.
- ▶ Now add that 'T' to the end of HEAR: HEART.
- ▶ We are left with hearing our own hearts, others' hearts and God's heart.

What a wonderful recipe, to be able to hear at a deeper level and live our lives that way. To allow ourselves to be less consumed by the negative, less boarded up, and to live more freely.

Your Ripple

Let's not be a cracked pot, fit only to be thrown out. Let's embrace the Kintsugi beauty intended for us.

Cracked pot, mad as a hatter or, as my stepdad would say, 'One sandwich short of a picnic!' does not appeal to me.

What about you?

If we leave the board around our heart and mind, then this is what we risk. It's not safer, is it?

I would like us to stop here and consider what needs to be taken care of.

What needs unblocking?
How can we guard our heart better without boarding it up again? Blind spots, as mentioned in the chapter 'A Friend or a Fraud', can be psychological, there to protect our hearts.

Chapter 7

Heart and Head Health

At times I feel that we live in a world where we may struggle to be the best we can be. I am therefore challenging us all to be that best, to do what we can to make the world a better place. I believe the creator of our universe intended it this way. If I am the best I can be, then I am my best for you. I can love, help, serve and support those around me to be their very best too. Surely then the world is more whole and more healthy?

As my family was falling apart and my heart was breaking, my loving, faithful dog Charlie was pressing in on me. My wonderful family was my everything, my world. I was hurting, crying. Charlie leaned in hard, reassuring me of his strong presence. He helped to take the pain away; that connection was real and loving. There was no need for words; just his presence. Animals love naturally and are so trusting; calm, like a mother nurturing her young.

Sadly, humans often become predators. Like animals, children naturally trust, unless that trust is broken by an adult. Then the damage reaches deep inside – it cannot be seen from the outside but it restructures the internal core and affects the person they were meant to be, creating instead a defended version of that beautiful, unique being. A newly created version, defending and protecting from the fear outside, and now inside – the self.

Sadly, this new self is the one now believed by the child, in order to survive, so that the child no longer recognises who they really are, lost until they reach a point in their life where they can search back to find themselves again.

From Five to Seventy-five

I have worked with five-year-olds and seventy-five-year-olds on this journey, and the issues are very much the same. Trapped inside, feeling like that tiny child, terrified to open up and 'be' themselves. It's terrifying to let the child 'be' again, so many are only half living.

I was once that child: broken, damaged, exposed, and I went on this journey to discover why and to work out who I really was without the damage and brokenness. I feared, like we all would, what we might find. I was nicely surprised, as you will be, at what I found: a kind, loving, friendly, family-orientated, intelligent and blessed person who I would not have believed I could be! I believed I wasn't capable of many things, including being academic enough to obtain a postgraduate degree or write a book. You will be surprised too – there is so much left to learn about yourself, given the opportunity!

You may well be staggered to realise that the person who irritates you the most could be just like you – reflecting your failings. And the person you most admire could demonstrate your best traits. It's all there too but maybe still to be discovered by you.

We can now look at areas that may be of concern. These issues come up regularly in my therapy room so may be of help.

Anxiety

We all know it and we all have it because it's a natural part of being alive. Some is actually good for us, like pain it is a warning sign. You may have heard of good stress; well, there are also good levels of anxiety. Sadly, lots of people live in the realm of the over-anxious. It is hard then to get excited about the possibility of a new way forward, or even to believe it can happen. I have clients who get excited about something new, but then anxiety and fear kick in to stop the process even getting off the ground.

Anxiety can cause migraines, vomiting, sensitivity to light and other environmental triggers, such as loud noises or flashing lights. If left unchecked, anxiety can lead to panic attacks and fainting. Living on the edge like this can make us prone to illnesses and will deplete the immune system over time. So it needs to be sorted out, put back into balance.

Good levels of anxiety, like other self-defence mechanisms, can drive us and even help us thrive. Left out of control, anxiety causes chaos for us and for others. In a post lockdown world we may well feel anxious, as life has changed for us all. It may never be the same again, so now is a good time to look at the effects of this on ourselves and on others.

One client I was helping had been taking drugs and came to me for help to stay off them. I started to work with him on tapping into his life dreams, as he was in his mid-twenties.

'I would love to write a book, but it's just a dream.'

'That's a really good goal. Why should it just be a dream?'

'I probably can't do it.'

'Have you told anyone that this is your dream?'

'No, because then when I can't do it I will let them down.'

The dream is dying before it even gets going, as the anxiety of letting others down is stronger than the desire to achieve it.

We looked together at this young man's past to see how we could turn this around and enable him to really live life and enjoy what he was made to do.

As we learn more about how the brain functions, we know there can be actual shutting down and cutting off. One young client I worked with, at the age of twelve was so cut off from his emotions that he could not feel excitement. For him, excitement would surge into anxiety and then the feeling that it could not be contained.

There may have been occasions when you have laughed until you cried and it was hard to contain yourself. That's just touching on this sense of losing control. There is a close correlation between excitement and anxiety shutdown and the impulsive nature we have when fear creeps in. Spontaneity, love of fun and enjoyment of a sense of freedom can all be stolen. This can then lead to a paralysis when it comes to making decisions in adulthood.

Adult clients who get stuck often say, 'I don't know what I want,' as they realise they have never got to know themselves or explored their dreams.

As they learn to talk through what it all feels like and give the emotions names, they begin to recognise the difference between emotion and anxiety, good and bad, fear and dread.

Panic attacks

These are what they say they are – attacks of panic. They catch us unaware and are hard to make sense of at the time. As I have worked on this issue with clients, I have found it helps to look at my own episodes in the past to see how panic attacks operate.

It may help to see panic as a character – a mass of colour and hair, with big eyes and a huge head that will just jump out of nowhere! Who created it, and how did it just arrive at work with me?!

Panic can arrive when we have pushed down the anxiety that has been growing over time. A sudden trauma can also bring it on. There is a sense of being out of control, of being fearful. Panic attacks are frightening and very unpleasant, as they lead to the feeling that the worst has happened.

I speak to clients about what would be the worst for them. Mostly it's embarrassment, humiliation and fear of being left alone. Addressing the root of these fears and what they really mean to each of us is vital.

There are many layers to every story, to every person's pain, and I am happy to hear and see these, to genuinely see someone for all that they are. I am yet to find a person who really is all the bad feelings and opinions that they have formed against themselves which bring on the anxiety or the panic. Anger and bad feelings become beliefs of 'I must be a bad person'. This is particularly sad when it is a child.

Talking, talking and more talking about the issues hidden within help to relieve the panic and anxiety, but you knew I was going to say that, I guess!

Sleep

If you have never had any sleep problems, then you have done very well. When sleep difficulties happen, it is often because our minds are full, and our thoughts circle around and around.

Are our minds trying to protect our hearts while our hearts try to protect our minds?

Our dreams can be unprocessed thoughts or fears. (Although, admittedly, sometimes they are totally random, often caused by a temperature, medication or cheese!)

What we have not worked through in the day can interrupt our sleep cycle. I offer dream interpretation and it is fascinating to work with this unconscious material. It can be hard to make sense of; what is protecting our minds can feel like it is damaging us, as those thoughts go around and around.

When life is going well, we find that there is less tension in our hearts and minds so we sleep better, eat better and generally things run as usual. However, many clients come in to see me because they are struggling with the basics of life and relationships. Some come because they feel there is something wrong that they cannot quite put their finger on. Many want to be like Dorothy in *The Wizard of Oz*, to click those shiny red shoes and be home and safe, a 'quick fix to put me right, please'.

Yet I have to say to that, no matter what your age, it has taken you your whole life so far to get to this point, so it may take a little time to work out what has happened on your journey and how you have survived.

We will cover gratitude later in this chapter, but just a heads-up on this . . . spending a little time before going off to sleep thinking positive and thankful thoughts is a wonderful way to unwind and drift off.

Nourishment

If we have a health scare, it may prompt us to start to take more notice of our diet and eating habits. But why wait for that moment; why not look now?

Oh, crumbs . . . to be the best you, let's have a look at what we are putting into ourselves. Is it simply what is available, is it what we have always eaten, or is it a well-thought-out, balanced diet? Why have the crumbs, not the best, when it's going into our bodies?

Having personally had a few health issues, I had to detox completely at one point as I had suspected Lyme disease. I was so sick I would have done anything to get well. It does take a shock sometimes to grab our attention. I was already eating well, but I had to really watch everything and listen to my body to figure out a way through.

Small changes can be the best, as I started to eat organic chicken instead as I was told chicken can be pumped with oestrogen. We will pay more in the short term, but gain more long term.

You do not need to wait for a shock like mine; we can start putting our food intake more into the forefront of our mind at any time. 'Heal' is in the word 'healthy', and our bodies are designed to heal themselves, so we are giving ourselves the best chance by taking a look at what we put into them. This is surely a good place to start making improvements to stay healthy.

Prevention is better than cure, right? This got me thinking . . . and taking a closer look at my fridge. I realised that many fruits and vegetables look like parts of the body . . . maybe this would be my way back to health?

- *Apples* – shaped like a brain and are good for our brains. (As are walnuts.)
- *Blueberries* – look like eyeballs and actually help the eyes.
- *Carrots* – cut, they also look like eyes. (You know where I am going with this . . . !)
- *Dates* – good for digestion and regular movements. (Don't let this put you off!)
- *Eggplant* – good for your heart; just take a look at the shape of it!

I could go on through the whole alphabet and many more fruits and vegetables, but I think you get the message: if we eat naturally and with knowledge, we can help our bodies stay well and hopefully heal themselves.

Creating Space

Let's not ponder for too long how many years have passed since those youthful runs around the fields with my friends and my dogs. So much has changed, mostly for the better, but some things are inevitably more challenging.

What strikes me as I recall my youthful escapades is how those primal experiences of communion – mind, body, spirit, soul and environment – have been replaced by disunity.

The quiet sense of running around the fields has been replaced by a world of digital media and devices. A broken, repetitive pattern of discord sadly keeps our attention. We have become about 'doing'.

'Just because it can be done, doesn't mean it should be done,' said a wonderful friend of mine. Let's hold that thought before we:

- Go, go, go.
- Do, do, do.
- Browse, browse, browse.
- Consume, consume, consume.

Instead, why don't we try the following (especially at a time when the world is rapidly changing – we can take this as an opportunity to do it differently):

- Breathe . . .
- Relax . . .
- Rest . . .
- Observe . . .
- Reflect . . .

So often the insistent 'Do, do, do' takes over again and we are left out of touch with the balance and quiet joy we once knew so well.

I smile at a memory of my lovely Josh when he was three years old as I found him sitting quietly in the garden.

Quiet children often make us worry – sad, but true!

It's no wonder we as adults do not know how to 'do' quiet!

I asked him,
  'What are you doing Josh?'

'I am having a piece of quiet, Mummy.'

I smiled and laughed inwardly. Earlier in that week he had
come and asked me what I was doing. I had said,
  'Having a bit of peace and quiet.'

Bless his heart; he learnt this quickly and in his early years.

So go ahead and enjoy your own 'piece of quiet'.

In Christian circles, we might think that our faith and
worldview would protect us from the machine-like message of
constantly doing more. There are many stories, symbols and
teachings in the Bible, and the practices of the Christian faith
caution us to pause and make time for God. Jesus said,
  'My yoke is easy and my burden is light' (Matthew 11:30).

I am challenging myself today as I challenge you. Find a space
in your day to stop and be. Take notice of what comes to mind.
Have a piece of paper ready to note down the inevitable 'to
do' things that will come to your mind, and then get back to
resting in him. Have your journal nearby too, to grab the gems
that come up: those things could be very relevant. Notice what
you feel in your body. Observe what flows around time and
time again. If 'being' is new to you, don't be surprised if you
find it difficult to start with.

Gentle music, being warm, having drink nearby and a view out of the window helps me to 'be'. Seeing birds, planes and clouds helps me listen. What helps you? Find the things that help you to be.

- ▶ Sit comfortably and take a deep breath, taking in your surroundings, and settle in the chair.
- ▶ Feel your feet upon the floor; sense the ground. Allow yourself to feel grounded.
- ▶ Then feel the chair holding you up, supporting your back. Relax into it and breathe.

Can we find the motivation to take down the board around our hearts? If life is good for us right now, can we encourage and help someone else?

As I get to help children do this through play, it enables them to work out their own emotions – to name them and understand them – and to become who they really should be. I asked one little lad of eleven,

'Does coming here to see me help you?'

'Yes, it's the only time I have space to settle my mind.'

It's such a privilege to help a child figure out their own way to become who they were created to be.

Creating Community
Being resourceful – using what's out there already

There are many great resources that can help us create space and also to create community so we can share time with others and grow with them. There is a list of recommended further reading towards the end of the book.

Count me in for accountability

As we listen to one another, we may find that things come to mind that need to be addressed. Being accountable to another person is a great place to start, then we can explore books, podcasts and other resources on the topic, and even seek pastoral or professional help.

Wonderfully multi-faceted

We are wonderfully multi-faceted human beings, and we can learn from all these aspects of ourselves:

- ▶ Physical
- ▶ Mental
- ▶ Emotional
- ▶ Spiritual
- ▶ Social

Considering all the aspects of ourselves, we can feel and sense when we are off kilter if we listen to our:

- ▶ Body – are we ignoring the signs it is giving us?
- ▶ Mind – are we revisiting something that needs attention?
- ▶ Heart – do we know something deep down but are not acting upon it?
- ▶ Spirit and soul – do we feel crushed or low?

As we are relational beings, when things go wrong it often shows through our communication with others.

Community and aloneness

Also relevant to all of us is the way we handle being alone, or the fear of being alone. This fear is a frequent visitor to my counselling room.

I studied many theorists while training, and Donald Winnicott was my centrepiece, my main man! His work changed many lives as he opened up a new way of helping people. His work on 'play' gave us much to think about when working with children and adults.

Donald Winnicott's *Babies and Their Mothers*, has given us even more to think about regarding aloneness: the state of being alone as an inevitable and ever-present aspect of a person's existence.[9] Understanding that it affects all of us as we look at our own way of being, can we be alone? Am I ever alone?

We learn this as a child: a totally dependent infant will be able to relax and even enjoy being alone on occasions. However, this will only be the case if there has been enough subliminally boundless support provided by a good-enough parent. But if this has not happened, the experience of being alone will be absolutely terrifying for the child. This is discussed in Winnicott's book, *Playing and Reality*, where he introduces the elegant concept of 'being alone in the presence of'.[10] In essence, if we were fortunate enough to be alone in the presence of our mother, then later in life we are able more easily to tolerate the experience of being alone. The fear will not be ever present or recurring, as I see happen for many as they seek to gain wholeness.

---

[9] Donald Winnicott, *Babies and Their Mothers* (Free Association Books, 1988).

[10] Donald Winnicott, *Playing and Reality* (Routledge Classics, 2005).

By 'wholeness', I mean a sense of being grounded, centred, focused and empowered.

It includes an ability to be spontaneous, heartfelt and creative. Those concerned are less likely to feel lonely and more able to be part of community.

Also relevant here is Winnicott's poignant,
'It is a joy to be hidden and a disaster not to be found.'[11]

So withdrawing, the need to be alone can be devastating if no one were to try to connect with you again. When someone is feeling hurt and withdraws, there is a risk that they may not be found or helped out of the isolation.

Belonging

At a conference at University College London (UCL), I was among neuroscientists and other psychotherapists as we explored attachment. It was fascinating to hear from the horse's mouth about belonging, and how community, or lack of it, can actually help or damage our brains physically. Proof from research, such as MRI scans, compared the brains of those who had been cut off from friends and loved ones with the brains of those who were regularly hugged and loved.

We all need a sense of belonging to keep ourselves healthy and more able to regulate our emotions. As we hug and are hugged, we produce oxytocin, which is naturally produced at birth with the bonding of mother and baby. It creates familiarity with those we affiliate with, and protection as we learn safety this way.

[11] Donald Winnicott, *Babies and Their Mothers* (Free Association Books, 1988).

Fathers produce oxytocin too – less than mothers, but they have it while they are close to the baby. When fathers go back to work, they are more likely to experience depression. It was agreed at the conference that fathers can experience postnatal depression. I was stunned to hear this. Is this why many relationships fall apart? Did my own parents' relationship fall apart because my dad was depressed? I guess it is good to be forewarned about this, so fathers can protect themselves, their partners and children at this stage of life.

It is certainly not an excuse for fathers to leave, to have an affair or to hit the bottle, but awareness is good so that we talk about it more. For men to admit that they are feeling low and to share their feelings is becoming more of an OK thing to do, thankfully.

I once had a client who was convinced that men could get postnatal depression. He believed he had it; he was a GP so he had medical knowledge. I do hope he finds some peace in discovering that his feelings were real and have been proven.

As oxytocin helps to create a secure base for us, it gives us security and helps us manage stress. Give hugs to your child, your family, your pets and your friends – increase their oxytocin levels while increasing your own.

Aloneness and attention

I see a client with relationship issues; she struggles with the belief that her partner's grown-up children exclude her.

'It feels deeper than rejection. For me there is a sense of being hidden. What is it about me that people seem to want to keep me hidden? Then I go into that place myself. I hide, isolate myself and withdraw.'

I see this often with clients. I have also known this pain myself, yet I do not live like it any more. I will purposefully put myself back into a social situation where possible. Yet the pain of being put there by another, of being controlled by another, is incredibly hard to manage. Anger, frustration and pushing away verbally and physically is the first instinct I might have. Yet if the act was done with a mature, balanced approach, would I handle it better? Would I manage better that sense of being controlled and hidden?

I need to unpack this part of my journey more. It started with having a father who left and a stepfather being present yet not reachable emotionally. I am being seen, yet not by my real father. He could not be there, and he was not at all aware of the damage being caused.

My stepfather was intermittent with his care. He was fun at times, but most of the time I was afraid of him. In front of others he was caring, but when they left he would push me off his lap. I found life confusing and frightening. My brothers would get beatings and I was told I would get 'a good hiding':
    'I will hit you so hard you will go out of the window.'

Maybe this was only said once, but every time I was shouted at I would look through the large window of our lounge, which was on the first floor of the house, and see the hard concrete below. I would imagine myself dead on the drive. It was terrifying to be disciplined in anger rather than managed in love. So, to me, anger became unbearable and ultimately meant death. I was taught not to cry, not to react and to 'be a good girl'. I wasn't sure I was a good girl but I tried very hard. So I learnt to hide my emotions as they were annoying to others. Consequently, who I was became hidden too.

Abuse can bring this same isolation and hidden defences. A child learns to believe there is 'something wrong with me', and this gets taken into the very core and becomes a self-belief. It's terribly sad and so wrong, but so common.

Going back to being hidden and hiding, once a person feels that control is coming back into play, it's hard to return from – but it is possible. Talking it out with the person is hard, but in that way it is possible to get to the root of it.

Admitting to a sense of feeling controlled when the other is not aware of their behaviour is very hard. Left to deal with it for ourselves, we need to recognise the pattern that will kick in. The isolation sets in and the pain of being rejected recurs. Yet if we know this is happening and allow ourselves time to recover, self-confidence can return and life can be restored.

Whether or not you decide to put yourself back into the ring for another round with the same person is up to you, but I would encourage you to pause and make a considered decision. Will the behaviour be repeated? Will there be room to explore what is going on for each person involved, or is it being kept hidden again?

This would be my question: am I being hidden or can I fully flourish in this environment?

I intend to live my life to the full, so I need to check whether I am allowing myself to do this and not finding myself back in a repeated cycle of pain. Not hiding but instead facing the pain is life-changing, yet so hard to do: I do not simplify this. The goal of changing needs to be acknowledged too.

On finding my biological dad, I discovered I had a sister and a brother, nieces and nephews. I also discovered a family tree going back generations to Italy, with noble roots! Finding a chronicle written by a family member back in the 1900s and referring back to the 1700s in Lucca, Milan and Florence was mind-blowing for me! I now had a sense of belonging and could keep researching the family tree. How amazing, when I was looking for one man, to gain such a legacy, as I discovered our family were pioneers and entrepreneurs. I learnt of their crossing from Italy, through Paris and then to London with their many talents and skills. It gave me more understanding of myself and my family who are still around.

Belonging is essential and wonderful. If we do not have it we can start to create it by joining groups and building it into our day to give the same familiarity.

So, facing the fear can be very rewarding. Even without rewards like these, it is worth it simply to not live under it any more. To have no shadow to come over and hide under is actually living in freedom. I personally have discovered a huge level of belonging and community that goes back in time, and I take forward this knowledge with me for the following generations.

Gratitude

Gratitude involves affirming the good in your life and recognising its source. It is understanding that life owes you nothing, that the good things are gifts that cannot be taken for granted. Research shows that gratitude truly felt can bring health benefits. It helps improve mental and physical health, increases life satisfaction, combats stress and much more.

The great news is that gratitude is easy. We can pick it up and put it down; it's available without cost. We can use it as we please. It cannot be overused, unless it is not authentic.

If thankfulness were a drug, it would be the world's best-selling product with a health maintenance indication for every organ of our body. It is known to:

- Lower blood pressure
- Lower blood sugar
- Reduce inflammation
- Reduce pain generally
- Improve heart health
- Relieve emotional distress
- Combat anxiety
- Combat mood swings and regulate mental health issues
- Improve sleep patterns
- Improve relationships

The key is to recognise the good and affirm the source. This links us to generosity, and to giving sacrificially. The good feeling after we help someone is scientifically proven to be linked in our brains. Caroline Leaf's detox programme includes thanksgiving, and it works very well. This then brings about a feeling of happiness.

Pay It Forward

Since the coronavirus outbreak, the world has changed. We have started to recognise our NHS workers as life-savers, and to see cleaners and other essential workers in a different light. Sports professionals and celebrities may not be as highly esteemed in the future as those who serve and save people.

The generosity of service by those who are prepared to give their all for others benefits everyone in so many ways, whether we see it or not.

Generosity may mean sharing your time, your home or your money; it may mean offering a sense of belonging, listening, or anything that you wholeheartedly feel you are putting out there for someone else. It is a way of gifting someone when you see a need, or simply want to bless someone.

Your brain can be changed in a lasting way as these positive actions sculpt its landscape and make new connections. This is a win–win: you help someone and they feel good; you are rewiring your brain, which makes you feel happier. You are creating something that is the opposite of a boarded heart – an open, healthy heart. It is the opposite of depression and feeling stuck, and you become freer to give and are open to receiving from others.

We can hold the worth of that ripple in our lives and see the changes that affect those around us. We can change forces that have come through the generations in our family – negative forces and patterns that have gone down the family line.

I would like to change the ripple that I send out, to be a message of hope:
    'I have worth and value, so do you.'

It is not about possessions or money. It's about recognising that each person is of unique worth. This is who I am and what I am about, and in turn I will value you and your family.

Abound In Boundaries

Creating healthy boundaries is good and necessary. Boundaries will always help us, no matter what stage of life we are in and what we have been through. When there has been abuse or trauma, it is hard to implement boundaries as they have been blurred by others. This can become hard to manage, and our boundaries can be easily broken. Knowing what they are and trying harder to keep them is very beneficial. Just as children need boundaries, so do adults, even though we might not like them, but we see the benefit of them in time.

Dr Henry Cloud has written a great book on boundaries if you feel you need to get further into this.[12]

When we are quiet about our boundaries, perhaps in an effort to seem more likeable, or to avoid conflict, we will become resentful, which will negatively affect our relationships, as well as our mental and physical health. Boundaries need to be clearly articulated, defined and enforced.

If you were to treat your personal boundaries like you treat the boundaries to your property (if you don't have one, just imagine having one), you would be much clearer about them, stronger about them and quicker to respond to any attack on them. In the same way, we must protect our relationships and our mental and physical health. We just need to view ourselves differently and act with clarity and positivity. Boundaries are not negative.

---

[12] Dr John Townsend and Dr Henry Cloud, *Boundaries* (Zondervan, 1992).

Being online and using social media can make it harder to enforce our boundaries. We used to be safe in our own homes, but now the atmosphere can change in an instant as a message pops up on our phone. We need to protect and guard ourselves, just like we physically protect our family, friends and property.

Gracelets

Here we can take some time to look at aspects of our lives that need attention. Anxiety can be isolated but may lead to issues with:

- ▸ Sleep
- ▸ Nourishment
- ▸ Creating space
- ▸ Community
- ▸ Gratitude

Finding hope in our lives and as we journey through can bring a renewed way of living: this I hope I can offer to you. Without hope we can lose our way and become sick. My hope comes from good support and from my faith in God, in myself and in others.

> Hope deferred makes the heart sick.
> *Proverbs 13:12*

Staying with good boundaries will help you to feel safer and secure, allowing you to enjoy life more freely and just to be.

Give a hug to your child, your family, your pets and your friends – increase their oxytocin levels and also increase your own. (Obviously where this is possible and safe.)

Find the things that help you just to 'be'.

Your Ripple

Where does your hope come from?

What comes to mind when you think of being alone? Can you be alone?

What mountain do you seem to go around?

Is there something that needs some attention from any of the areas we have looked at: anxiety, sleep issues, food issues, being alone, being with others and being able to be grateful?

Are you hiding in some way a part of your life or a part of yourself? Would it help to find this for yourself or to be found by another?

Are there areas of your life that need better boundaries, for your own well-being and that of others around you?

Chapter 8

My Secret Weapon

Turning our weaknesses into strengths can really be an incredible journey. My experience of not knowing myself emotionally, added to the anxiety I experienced from undiagnosed dyslexia, meant I had a long way to go. Many of us don't know why we feel what we feel, and I use dyslexia as a good example of this. It brings confusion and frustration, like many other hidden issues we may have.

My dyslexia, which I call my brilliant secret weapon, seemed to be my enemy for my entire school life and until I discovered I had it when I was in my forties. It came with no title; it was a secret kept from me as well as from everyone else. It came with no introduction or warning. Was it always there? Did I inherit it?

I believe dyslexia occurs during early development if the nurturing process is interrupted. It tends to come down the mother's side if it is inherited yet there is no exact science in this as far as I know.

Main differences for those with dyslexia is our cortex is wired differently, it could be said that it malfunctions. The cerebral asymmetry is different also which means we process information on the right side of the brain, this would usually be the left side. This can mean that concepts are understood more easily when communicated in pictures as it is hard for the thoughts to be processed and communicated.

This can slow down the process of information. This is a general description and can vary from person to person.

It does not mean we are not smart, just doing it differently, we are actually processing far quicker because we are creating images. We tend to be more creative, however we do have to work harder with our short-term memory; recalling directions, for example, can be near impossible! If there are no images to link the words to then it is hard to hold onto them. Give me one or two and I'm good but three and it's all over!

It does not mean we do not like reading or enjoy words, even though they can get muddled on a page; we can miss words and lines out. We may have to re-read to grasp the content. However, we may still love to learn and read but struggle with it. There is a tendency to get tired and give up.

I found out that I had dyslexia in the last trimester of my postgraduate diploma in counselling when I was almost unable to read, it was like I had forgotten how to. I was sent for a test which showed I had covered it up by teaching myself to speed read. This was somehow working until I hit the complicated words in my psychotherapy books and my flow was lost. I would read each word at a time, forget the whole sentence and have to start again. I was given tinted glasses, computer software and a few other props and gadgets, then off I went again . . . it was amazing!

I have it, it's not going away but can be made easier. I am now secretly using it every day of my life. Well, it was my secret until I am now sharing it with you. When I couldn't identify it, it would plague me every day.

Dyslexia: my secret weapon – my friend, my enemy, my failing, my challenge, my energy, my inspiration, my drive, my creativity; all mine to do what I want with. I no longer live under it but instead I choose to soar on its wings, and I would like to take others with me.

As I gained understanding about my uniquely wired brain (I used to think and say 'dodgy' – now I know better!), I learnt how specular it is! If not discovered, dyslexia is a hidden enemy, like a shadowy figure ready to stick a foot out in front to trip us up at any time. Even now, even when I am feeling confident, I might trip over a word or a meaning, or I'm unable to process my thinking or my words quickly enough. I could spell a word one day and it's gone the next.

As I started my counselling practice more and more clients came who showed emotional and mental health issues that I could tell many were struggling with dyslexic tendencies. It can affect someone in how they organise themselves, time-keeping and staying with a topic of conversation due to our brains working so fast. This means we can jump from topic to topic very quickly, most annoying probably for others. Other aspects that can come with dyslexia are anxiety, fear, lack of self-confidence and even suicidal thoughts. It so needs to be known, not left misunderstood but enhanced. For me it has felt like someone is watching, just waiting to step out and trip me up at any moment. They would find out that I cannot really do it, whatever it is. Knowing this can happen I now talk it out with someone. I hear myself getting in my own way before they even have to say anything. Then I go at it again, such as this book, otherwise it would be my own thoughts, mind and self-believe that is most likely to stop me rather than anyone else getting in the way.

Blown Away

I experienced a massive blow. I met a very attractive man and we got on really well. Then, after a second date, he texted me to say he didn't feel right because he had noticed that I paused before I spoke and it made him feel uncomfortable, so he didn't feel he could have a relationship with me. I was mortified, so much so that I decided not to explain about my dyslexic tendencies. I could have explained that this happens from time to time, but it doesn't mean I am daft or hiding something! If I had received the consideration from him to talk to me and to find out how I tick, I would have had the opportunity to say what this is like for me. It felt punishing and terribly sad to be dropped with little attempt to understand rather than being given a chance to explain.

Since then I have decided that dyslexia will not stop me having a relationship, running a business or helping others, because I am happy to tell anyone about it, given the chance. Get it out there into the light. It's not an excuse, but it is about awareness for those who think it's only about muddling up our Bs and Ds. Dyslexia is far more of a dangerous weapon against us when it's unknown and undetected, but it can be a powerful tool when it's embraced and cultivated.

For children and young people at school, dyslexia can cripple and maim an education if it is not recognised. It can cause frustration as a result of seeming ongoing failure, and many dyslexics can end up involved in antisocial behaviour as they try to manage the tension of it. Stress and insecurity partner together and can take you down.

Negative feelings can be formed early on, as dyslexics don't fit in well into a well-crafted system of non-dyslexics.

Patterns are formed from an early age as we battle to not fail and to manage something that might take us down at any moment.

Discovering what we are good at is key to managing these thoughts and feelings. Having kind and loving people around us helps beyond words. Understanding friends and family members save us from ourselves. To put it bluntly, it's hard work for us, so if you are able to understand us then it saves us digging even deeper to find a way to express ourselves when this is so difficult for us already!

Struggles Within; Privilege to Help

A fourteen-year-old girl was referred to my counselling practice. She was suicidal, that's all I knew. She arrived and I was shocked! She was so beautiful, with a gorgeous slim figure and long, shiny hair down to her waist. Her delicate features looked so sad and uptight.

It took me only ten minutes to see that she had such a severe case of dyslexia that her short-term memory was shot. She couldn't remember much at all. Imagine studying for exams with very little short-term memory.

To make it worse, the poor girl would sit with her friends and they would share a memory and laugh, but she would sit there and feel as though she hadn't been there. This is like having dementia at the age of fourteen! My heart went out to her, and I invited her to go online to the British Dyslexia Association website. She scored highly in the online test for dyslexia.

I began to counsel this girl, and she became happier in school as they were able to help her once her dyslexia had been diagnosed. We worked on her self-esteem, helping her realise her dreams and desires. Eventually she went off to college. I am not saying she lived happily ever after, but receiving a diagnosis and counselling helped her to be more self-aware. Her confidence will inevitably go up and down, even though she looks a million dollars. She will struggle in her studies, but now she knows a lot more about what's happening to her and why.

This is self-empowering; it's not a label to hide behind but rather a superpower to rocket her into being fully herself. She now knows she can be a beautician without fearing judgement and assumed to be stupid because she struggles to remember things, and actually her memory is improving because she is less anxious.

If you have dyslexia or dyslexic tendencies, diagnosed or undiagnosed, I hope this has helped you so far. Or you may have other weaknesses that can be turned into strengths. I have not met a perfect person yet, so there is bound to be something that will cause you some area of discomfort or anxiety. Please don't just put up with it; talk it out with someone and see how it can transform your life, and maybe even someone else's life too.

You may have experienced a bereavement or crisis, then you find that others start talking to you because you understand their pain. There is an opening, a sense of your world not being perfect and sorted.

You have been through something difficult, which allows others to share their own difficulties and vulnerabilities. Embracing problems and issues can turn them on their heads.

Left unheard and unhealed, such challenges can lead to mental health issues and even suicidal thoughts, as it's hard work to manage them day in, day out. However, embracing the beast, taming it and transforming it into a friend turns it into power. It's now a brilliant secret weapon to recognise as an asset to use creatively as you roll with its ebbs and flows. Laugh at the funnies it creates and lighten your heart with the fun you can have with it.

Meeting the Dragon Again

You may remember my adventure with Rachel Elnaugh. Well, as I mentioned briefly, more came from that meeting, as she became my business mentor.

As a result of retreating regularly to our friends' house in Somerset, running retreats was really on my heart. Their home just happens to be next to the Glastonbury Festival site, which for most of the year is simply miles of countryside – until the event happens. Our quiet retreat, our friends' house, became for others a thriving music festival in June!

I sat with Rachel in her garden, on a soft sheepskin rug. Little did she know how this would tap straight into my soul. My earliest memory is of touching such a rug. I could hardly see, yet no one knew, so touch was vital to me. I would pull funny faces, probably trying hard to see my family. They would laugh, so I would laugh. This led them to believe I was a happy baby.

What they didn't know then was that, when I was born, I was extremely long-sighted and also had a squint. My grandfather picked up on my squint and my eyesight was then tested, and I began to wear glasses at the age of two.

So, as I sat on this rug, I felt good, held emotionally by Rachel. She encouraged me to share my dream. I laughed, as I felt it was too extreme, too indulgent, too big even for a Dragon from *Dragons' Den*!

I started to paint the picture, which unfolded as we spoke:
    'Well, it has an infinity pool set in hills or mountains. I see animals because they are so healing. It's accessible for wheelchairs so it can be a place of respite for families. Many rooms allow space away, and there are rooms set up for counselling, reading or just to "be" with a lovely view.'

'So why can't you have that?'

'Well, it probably doesn't exist,' I laughed.

'Well, it might, and then you could have more around the world, not just one.' With that, I laughed even more.

Only two months later, I visited some friends in Spain and arrived at their newly rented place. We travelled up and up the mountain to a gated community and into a gated property. On a quick tour before dinner, I realised I was seeing the place I had visualised. I couldn't tell anyone as I was so stunned. This was their place, they were millionaires – how could this become a retreat centre? And they were only renting it anyway.

This is the first time I am telling this story; my friends do not know I had visualised this place as I was so astounded at the time. Rachel had strengthened my thinking, my mind and my expectations. Why should I not dream big? Dyslexia did not stop Richard Branson – it may well have made him who he is today.

Richard Branson was involved in a video in support of Made by Dyslexia. Once you get to see the website and watch the video showing who else in the world has it or was believed to have had it, you may even be jealous of not having it! It appears that companies are beginning to actively employ at least one dyslexic, as we bring such creativity and think out of the box. You need us guys!

Kate Griggs, who set up Made by Dyslexia, has a team who interview people about their thoughts about dyslexia – you can see it on YouTube or TED Talks.[13] The person interviewing on the streets says something like,
   'What would be your reaction if you found out your baby had dyslexia?'

One reaction was,
   'Well, I wouldn't kill it!'

How shocking, and what a relief!!

On many levels I found this reaction scary. That we feel that something viewed as 'wrong with us' can be so misunderstood.

---

[13] http://madebydyslexia.org (accessed 19 May 2020).

That abortion could be considered so freely to get rid of a person simply because of their differences.

Why would such a thing even be said? It would be killing off such qualities as:

- ▶ Tenacity – dog-with-a-bone kind of determination!
- ▶ Stamina
- ▶ Creativity
- ▶ Focus – we produce amazing results if you bear with us!
- ▶ Ability to see the bigger picture
- ▶ Entrepreneurship
- ▶ Empathy

Does this make you think of your own qualities and strengths?

I hope so.

Biggest Challenge Yet!

Getting inspirational thoughts onto paper is one of the most challenging parts of the writing process for me. My book has taken years because of the fear that I will not be able to put into words what I am sensing without it losing its impact, its power, its original context and meaning.

I fear the words will lose their sparkle by being pinned to the paper, like a butterfly trapped, crumpled and pinned by its wings.

No longer alive.

Brutalised.

There is a sense of something being stolen away before it even exists – my thoughts, sharp and true, inspiring and new . . . then gone in a flash.

Will they ever reappear or exist again?

However, I have kept going with my writing, and I will keep going despite the challenges I face.

As well as this I find it difficult to retain numbers and to add them up in my head, but I manage to counsel people and do my accounts. Nothing is impossible; it's just harder work. Just knowing that 40 per cent of self-made millionaires are dyslexic helps me to keep going (currently about 10 per cent of the overall population are dyslexic, although many could still be undiagnosed).

I want to champion others and help those who find it hard to read. Ensuring that our publishing house is 'dyslexic friendly' has been essential. Then, at a publishing conference in Nashville, I met a typographer, which gave me the chance to fulfil my dream of making reading easier for everyone, especially dyslexics. So we have been working on producing a new font, called Grace. This is the font you are reading now! (I hope you are or something has gone wrong at the last hurdle!)

Nashville: More Than a Song

I arrived for the conference in Nashville not knowing what to expect. I heard a great talk from Klaus Krogh, a typographic designer, then we all headed off to workshops.

I found myself in a talk by Klaus that he appeared to be repeating from the introduction. Far too polite and English to walk out, I decided to engage with his theme. He spoke about creating familiarity with typefaces; a familiar style will welcome someone back.

Behind this was the story of reading. Human beings were not designed to read words; they were humanity's creation that developed from pictures. This made sense to me, as someone for whom reading came so hard. It's not a natural activity; we have made it that.

Being interested in neuroscience, I was fascinated by Klaus's understanding of how our brains work as we read. We fire off neurones in reaction to something new, then, as it is repeated, it starts to make sense to us: 'I know this', whether we know it or not.

Having heard Klaus's talk already, my instinct was to check my reaction to it. It was a good experience so I decided to apply what he was teaching. I started to identify with it, and it immediately seemed easier to understand it.

At the end of the workshop, Klaus recognised me from his earlier talk. I shared with him what I had done while I was listening to him. I am not proud of making a grown man cry, but he did!

'I go around the world telling people about this and you just did it!' he said to me.
It was a great feeling and a great outcome.

'We should do some work together!' Klaus said.
'Great. What shall we do?' I replied.

'I would love my own dyslexic font,' I sighed with praying hands.

'Great! Let's do it!'

So now you are reading the outcome of this meeting. What a wild wing of adventure life can be when we think and act outside the box. I love it!

Showcase

There is so much I could tell you about the bringing of this font into being, but that is really another story altogether.

However, I will share with you the reactions of a group of dyslexic children in two schools where we tested it. This was their feedback:

Instant Impact

Isabella (dyslexic): 'It was much better. Usually words go all wonky for me but in this book the boldness made the words stand out more which made it easier to read.' Isabella has since discovered that a greenish overlay aids her reading ability.

Jayden (undiagnosed with dyslexic tendencies): 'The book was good. I read it faster than normal. Probably because the writing was a bit bigger. It was better this time because I didn't skip lines.'

Muwahhid (undiagnosed with dyslexic tendencies): 'At the start it was easy to read and I wasn't skipping any words. I was reading faster than usual as it was really easy to see. Near the end I started to skip a bit. But the words are more clear than other fonts.'

Cristian (dyslexic): 'I thought this book was better as the writing helped me to read it. The words were not joined which sometimes happens with words in other typefaces. Usually when I read I skip a line, but with this writing I didn't skip any lines and I read it a lot faster!'

Sabrina (dyslexic): 'I liked the text. It was much easier to read, and the background colouring helps that it is not just black and white.

Also the images in the book were big and vibrant which makes it more enjoyable and helps with what you are reading.'

Kate (language and communication difficulties): 'When I was reading this book it did seem a bit quicker to read and also it was a lot more fun to read this typeface and the content of the book. I prefer reading in this typeface to usual typefaces in books.'

Tabitha (dyslexic): 'Well, it's easier to follow it along and I don't miss words or lines and they don't move. But it still took me a while to figure out the word. The blue paper made it quicker to read in general too.'

Abi (teacher): 'The students were so much more responsive during your presentation than I expected. They are all students who have some level of learning difficulty and can be reluctant to participate at times. It is really promising to witness them engage in a topic that instantly impacts on their ability to participate. The fact that they can recognise that the typeface "Grace" makes a difference to their reading ability is amazing and has given them confidence.'

When we received this feedback from the schools, it made Klaus cry again – and it got me too! We could not have asked for more! To think that we can change their reading experiences, which will change their lives. Without the right knowledge and support, many of these children will feel left behind and anxious, which may lead to mental health issues.

Yet creating the group gave them a new sense of belonging: we understand each other; we get it! They can now recognise each other around school and hopefully help each other out.

Identity is key for us all, but especially when there is an issue that feels hard to pin down. Seeing others manage it can help to bring about a new identity. We have this, but it's OK, and we can work it to our advantage – it has its strengths as well.

I will share a little of Klaus's story if I may:

A Dyslexic Typeface

Long before I could read, I was deeply fascinated by letters, by these transformed pictograms, made into abstractions, which denote sounds and which can be put together into words, beautiful words. These beautiful words most of us learn to recognise by the thousands, even if they are dressed up in different typefaces.

But not me. When I started in school, it very soon became evident that I was dyslexic. When my teacher told me, he kindly said,
　'It is not the end of the world!'
The sentences that followed that statement, however, which I have luckily forgotten, clearly indicated that it was pretty close to 'the end of the world'.

My strategy? I decided to love these beautiful words even more. I loved them so much that I started to create typefaces. I created the first one when I was thirteen, so that I could write 'Bob Dylan' on my wall. When I had letters enough to carry out the project, I kept on designing.

Fulfilling the alphabet then became an important task. Today I am, as one of the 40 per cent of dyslexic entrepreneurs, the CEO of a type foundry, typographic design and typesetting company called 2K/Denmark. To become our very best, we use the knowledge obtained by research into how a reading brain works. We know that for a word to be 'read', it first has to be recognised in the lower part of the brain. That is the same place we recognise faces and facial expressions. But from there it has to be transported to the central part of the brain to be recognised as language. That is the connection we have to establish when we learn to read. We have to rewire our brain.

Humans are not born readers, but we are born speakers and listeners. When we listen to sound, it goes directly into the central part of the brain, where it is recognised as language. Around 430 AD, St Ambrose, Bishop of Milan, was a notability. St Augustine said about him, 'When he reads his eyes scanned the page and his heart sought out the meaning, but his voice is silent and his tongue is still.' By this, we are led to believe that St Ambrose was the first man who relinquished the detour around speech and hearing and made his brain create the connection directly.

So what better use of our knowledge and design capabilities than to try to create a typeface to help dyslexics to recognise beautiful words more easily?

Inspired by a lady who had face blindness to the degree that she could not recognise herself in the mirror in the morning before she had put on make-up, I had the idea to create a typeface with make-up on.

Emphasising the personality of each letter and distinguishing those that look most alike. Not to make it pretty, but to help to create new, more recognisable wordscapes (collections of letters still to be understood as a word).

NOTICE! Reading this text using the font will, in the beginning, feel more difficult, but I think that once you have got used to it, it will gradually become more and more easy to recognise the wordscapes and to convert them into an understanding of beautiful words.

Klaus E. Krogh, Type Founder
2K/TYPOGRAPHIC DESIGN

Helping You to Help Me

Helping you to help me – this is where we need family and friends to understand the effects of dyslexia. To learn about it, understand how it really is for the person who has it, accept it and explain it to others. Being understood and not being criticised or pressured can help a dyslexic to really blossom emotionally, rather than to wither. We can have fun with it if we feel understood, otherwise it becomes a weapon used against us, which will obviously make a person shrink away. To enable a person to blossom, there is plenty of room for encouragement and acknowledgement on our good days – as well as on the more difficult days, of course!

Doing the Detox

Having mentioned Caroline Leaf's 21-day detox and how it helped me personally, it also helped me on my writing journey.

It felt as though it decluttered my mind so I was ready to write. It helped me to detox a toxic thought that was profoundly affecting me.

The detox (book or app) worked for me by starting my day listening to the video, then working on a toxic thought replacing it with a positive thought. Caroline, a neuroscientist, encourages us by reading the thought many times during the day so I put prompts in my diary. Saying it out loud was powerful and a great reminder of what I was working on. The active reach, she calls this, it actively engages us with the rewiring of our brains. She encourages us to journal, keep specific with our thoughts and this helps us gain awareness of our thinking. This causes structural changes in our brain affecting our body, mind and spirit.

I am currently feeling as though some of the more challenging aspects of my dyslexia are improving! I hope to remain with its positive effects, particularly my creativity, as I am working this part of my brain by designing book covers and writing. I am expanding my concentration by working a little longer each time I feel like getting off my seat. Allowing myself to take breaks has always helped, and that's OK too. Yet the negative aspects of jumping from one topic to another, being unable to visualise words and type them, say them and spell them have been reducing. I am keen to see if this continues.

If we are living life in all its fullness, then we are good to be around. We find our talents and gifts as we live in this way, and we have them to share with others.

Whether that is running an alpaca farm in the Cotswolds so that the wool can be used for beautiful and practical things, or being a top chef, or taking a risk to attend a very small retreat to bless a few people: these things can change the world. The chef will feel fulfilled as everyone enjoys their creativity, and the people will be well nourished and feel taken care of. For the person attending the conference, the ripple effect may only be in the moment of togetherness, or it may ripple out to others as they go home and share how they managed to write the next part of a children's book. This book may be inspiring to just one child or to many. The child may grow up to become a well-known speaker on an inspiring topic, and so many are hugely blessed by a small act.

As I started my own 21-day detox, a deep fear of being left alone and being left behind came so clearly into focus it was scarily real. I realised I could actually start to believe there was no way out. But I knew I no longer had to live with this feeling.

I have told you already that I grew up with five older brothers, so this feeling of aloneness was ever present. I could not keep up, and being the only girl, being left out was usual. It hurt, and this would reappear as a pattern of vulnerability throughout my life. To work on this meant really digging deep and facing how it had held me back and affected my relationships. Yet at the same time I was seeing that its grip was easing – could I really let it go? Even as a therapist and having worked tirelessly to move through my own stuff, this was my nemesis. Could this really work? Could I see it through? I so wanted to better myself, both for my own sake and to know with my hand on my heart that I could help a client or author through this too.

Renewing Our Mind

Having been steered to Caroline Leaf's material and then hearing her speak on rewiring the brain, I felt as though my prayers had been answered. I had been exploring whether it is possible to speak ourselves into sickness, such as dementia, and maybe then I could work myself out of my dyslexia issues. I heard Caroline speak and then I spoke to her husband, who blessed me with further material to help me discover this fully. Having this validated was like a light-bulb moment for me: this wasn't me just wondering whether it was possible, as Caroline had actually done it and written heaps about it. Fantastic! Now I could really run with it.

Now, how does this relate to dyslexia? Well, for me, the anxiety that was created by dyslexia added to the anxiety created by my position in the family. Not being able to learn to read quickly enough, or to process and recall what I was reading quickly enough and trying hard to get my words out in a big, busy family often left me trying but mostly failing. I became shy and often tearful with frustration. I began to believe I had nothing to give and would never catch up or be the same. As a girl, I couldn't be the same as my brothers, and I began to see my differences as negatives. A lot of teasing added to my lack of self-worth.

I do not remember being told I was pretty or beautiful; just too loud, too quiet, stupid or annoying. Along with undiagnosed dyslexia, I now know that it was a hard slog just to be a girl in a male-dominated world, as I would try to say how I felt and it was not going to be received anyway.

My secret weapon had been my enemy for all my school years and for all of my life, until I found out about it not that long ago.

However, now I know about it, I am using this weapon every day of my life. It can sometimes be hard to process my thinking or my words quickly enough, and many aspects can be difficult. Yet I see that I am in tune with others, and I am creative.

I'm happy to tell anyone about my dyslexia and how it affects me, and to help others discover whether they have it.

Learning about ourselves emotionally can be a tricky journey at the best of times; trying to navigate this alone or within a relationship can be the most experiential trip we will take. Not knowing what is happening with our emotions is hard enough, even though awareness of mental health issues is on the rise, but for those with dyslexia anxiety, this is a biggie. Many of us don't know why we feel what we feel, so I use dyslexia as a good example. Many people do not like to have a diagnosis for fear of others thinking that they might use it as an excuse. I cannot stress enough what a difference it makes to know why we do what we do. Dyslexia is a brilliant example of this, as it's there all the time and differs from day to day.

Gracelets

I call my dyslexia a weapon because of my belief in how powerful it is. I have decided I want to use it to soar and I would like to take others with me.

If you want to soar or are soaring, what does that look like for you?

Do you have an entrepreneurial spirit? Do you:

- ► Think about new products that could be developed?
- ► Recognise gaps in the market?
- ► Always look to see what is needed?
- ► Want to collaborate to see change?

Try the detox basics. I recommended one minute each of:

- ► Thankfulness
- ► Praising
- ► Worshipping

> God has made you uniquely you.
> He knows the plans he has for you!

Your Ripple

What is your struggle?

What would your weapon be?

This is self-empowering, not a label to hide behind but a superpower to rocket you into being fully yourself.

What would you rather call it, if not a weapon?

What do you think could stop you reaching your goals or having a go at things?

Do you think there is something in your life that pops up time and time again and needs to be taken care of? Do you need to talk that out with someone, or take more determined steps to get a diagnosis?

What is stopping you moving out of your comfort zone?

If there is nothing that needs looking at, is there a way that you could help others?

Just knowing that 40 per cent of self-made millionaires are dyslexic helps me to keep going. How about you?

What would stop you helping others?

Chapter 9

True Colours

I have learnt some really powerful lessons from many clients and friends. One person who taught me a lot was my friend Paul, who I introduced in an earlier chapter. 'Such a gentle man,' was how he was described by so many. I believe he taught me what a true gentleman is. I had not seen it displayed in everyday life before. It was the essence of who he was; he was a treasure to all who knew him. I had the pleasure of meeting him just before I got married and he was in and out of my life along the way. I somehow always knew he was there even if I did not see him for a long time. He worked as a postman and would bring a happy smile with my letters. Just the fact that he was there was lovely to know. Don't we all need that?

On one of our last days together we watched *Jungle Book*, on a wet Sunday afternoon, eating popcorn, lying on his hospice bed. I couldn't help thinking how Bagheera and Baloo were always there, looking out for Mowgli, trying to deliver him to the best place for him. All the fun, care and help they gave to Mowgli was directed towards a much greater goal – that Mowgli could go to a better place, away from the dangers of the jungle, and have a peaceful life in the village with his own kind.

Everyone who met Paul knew he was a joker, just like Baloo, always seeing the funny side, and he was caring too.

He was there when times were good and when they weren't. It was the simple things in life he liked, the 'bare necessities of life'.

Paul was very supportive of my publishing. He would buy books and sell them to friends and nurses in the hospice, and he would tell me how proud he was of me.

Paul was much loved by all who knew him. One of the things that blew us away was how his fellow workers did his work for him to keep his pay going while he was sick. They covered his shifts so his pay would keep coming while he was receiving treatment for cancer. What a testimony of his character and the love they had for him! He simply gave and loved, and this was returned to him. His ripple was simple yet deep.

He had gone through life mostly enjoying the journey. At one time he hit a bad patch and shut his emotions down to protect his broken heart. I hoped and prayed he would open up and that his body would respond too. But it was already shutting down as the cancer was taking over. He started to listen to his heart and his body improved, but it was too late to beat the cancer.

He had resigned himself to dying.
'I have had a happy life,' he told me.

Yet as we spent time together, watching films or taking little trips out, he seemed to keep going far beyond the months he had been expected to survive. He was outstanding in his ability to cope with the pain and kept smiling throughout. He loved a giggle and made all the nurses laugh. They loved him, as we all did.

I was just about to take him away on a trip to Spain for a holiday when he had a fall and had to be taken into the hospice. It was a shock and I rushed to see him. He had a side room with a bathroom and a nice view.

'Fancy booking your own holiday without me, and a room with a view all to yourself,' I joked.

'Well, you'd better go home and get your toothbrush.'

When I came back later that evening to see him I brought my toothbrush and put it next to his. It was my way of letting him know that I was there for him and all was not lost, even though the holiday could not happen. It had been a lovely distraction for a while. He joked about me trying to get him up the hill in a wheelchair and told me to start working out for the grand trip!

Many times it was hard to know what to do for Paul, especially when he was in the hospice. Everything he needed was pretty much there for him, so I learnt to just be there. It may not have felt like I was doing much, but I quickly learnt that I was. Having had him in my life has enriched and helped me, and being there for him in his last year was a privilege, I am so blessed to have had that time with him.

I learnt what pure love is: no physical complications, just being there and loving someone for who they are. His colours truly shone out – I think even more so towards the end of his life. I am better for having known him, yet it hurt to let go . . . just like Baloo and Bagheera letting Mowgli go, but knowing it was the right time for him.

Paul promised to look down and take care of me, wanting to protect me and to be there. This on many occasions has given me comfort. I know he is now in a peaceful place, like Mowgli. Yet I would have preferred to have him here. He knew me well enough to know what I needed: a partner who shared my faith, to journey with.

The sadness of shutting down our emotions not only stops us feeling them; it does way more damage than that. Understandably, it can feel as though they are going to fill us up and overwhelm us at times. The fear of them killing us off or killing off another can be an unconscious power behind the scenes.

I have worked with a number of clients within a hospice setting. Many relatives have somehow taken on that they had something to do with the person dying. This can be especially true of children:

'If I had been better behaved my dad may still be here,' said one child, fearing that it was his anger that had killed his father.

Emotions have more impact on our bodies than we may give them credit for. Being brave and facing the fears that come up gives us the power back. Our goal should be to face and then embrace them and show them who's boss! Then we can truly shine out our true colours!

So to truly let our true colours shine we may need to take a look at a more holistic approach to life. To really engage in all aspects of life is a challenge. We like to focus on areas that are familiar to us.

If we are used to going to the gym to let out our frustrations, we might focus on that and not consider that we are spiritual beings. Or we may be so involved in church life that we do not get enough physical exercise. Finding and keeping a balance is one thing, but actually becoming aware of all our needs in the first place is a key step.

Are we really taking care of ourselves in a wholesome way? Each of us is a whole person, and it is important that we hold in mind the bigger picture of all aspects of our multi-faceted selves:

- Physical
- Emotional
- Mental
- Spiritual
- Social

Let's look at these individually.

Physical Needs

It is good to take a look at what we may require physically in our day-to-day, as well as in the long term. Under normal circumstances, many of us live in a place of rush. Crisis management and plate spinning; dashing from one event to another is the norm. Have you ever heard yourself say, 'When it is calmer next week I will take care of that . . .'?

But then we were all put on pause, as though Bill Gates had pressed Alt, Control, Delete on the mainframe of the world. We were told to stop. We are not wired to do this, so how do we do that without anxiety and frustration kicking in?

We have been told by our government that exercise once a day is good for us. Now it's official – we can go ahead and do it. Having been told it is essential, we allow ourselves to do it whereas we otherwise may not have.

The world continues to change and evolve, continually finding a new normal. As this happens, what is the way forward?

I have a plan that I try to stick to as best I can: to make one personal appointment for myself each week. It may be a dental appointment, the doctor or dog grooming. In this way, a practical issue is solved each week, which saves a build-up. Having appointments booked ahead used to stress me, but now I have a plan I am much calmer. We have probably all heard about 'me time', and that is important too. I have told you about the spa I am a member of, and I put my visits there into the diary too.

This way of managing things keeps them flowing and doesn't put too much pressure on my diary. Once things are in place it has become a plan that has just taken shape, so I do not have to think about it too much.

Working out what your physical needs are and taking care of them is the most sensible thing to do, yet many find it difficult to put themselves first. As discussed earlier, it is like the oxygen mask on a plane: we are told to take care of our own breathing so that we are able to help another. We are not much help if we cannot breathe!

Taking a walk, getting fresh air, getting back to the gym, riding a bike, flying a kite: anything that allows a bit of freedom and exercise is good for the whole body.

So, too, is considering what you eat and drink. Consuming enough vitamins will help to boost your immune system so eating a healthy diet and, if necessary, taking supplements regularly is all important.

Emotional Needs

This area I wanted to put top of our list, but we need to be practical and check that our physical needs are being met. Emotional needs vary from person to person, so it does take time to figure out our own needs. Working with a counsellor is a good way to really unpack this. However, you can assist yourself along the way just by taking the time to think about things and bring your emotional awareness into sight.

When our emotions are out of balance, it can be very exhausting, so it is worth considering how well you are doing emotionally as this will impact you mentally and physically.

Mental Needs

Staying healthy mentally can be helped in many ways, whether we feel a bit pressured or even pushed to the edge. To keep the balance, it can help to write down your dreams and desires, how you might like to be living day to day. Make a point of journalling when something comes into your awareness.

We also need to be aware of how much information we are taking in from the television and social media. The impact of bad news can be more draining on us mentally than we realise. If we limit ourselves to listening to the news once a day, we remain in control of it. We can also limit the news feeds that flash up on our smartphones.

We might believe it doesn't affect us, but it is subtle as it seeps in and then checking it becomes a habit. Let's be aware and in control of what we allow in.

Spiritual Needs

I talk about my faith in every area of my life, so it is natural for me to talk about it in this book. Wherever you are on your spiritual journey – exploring, or a strong, mature believer leading others along the way – knowing that you are continuing to move forward is important.

Being shut down spiritually means there is an area of your life still not really known and enjoyed as I believe it could be. One of the most exciting moments of my life was seeing Jesus; I had no doubt it was him. I know not everyone will have an experience such as this; your journey will be different. Just allowing yourself to look is the first step, and the most exciting is what is yet to come.

One exciting book I have been a part of publishing is Martin Young's *This Is That*.[14] Martin and I chatted with great excitement about those 'this is that' moments. I call them divine appointments, when you just know that this is an encounter that God has organised. If we look and listen we can recognise these wonderful moments and see, feel and enjoy as we connect spiritually.

---

[14] Martin Young, *This Is That* (Malcolm Down Publishing, Nov 2020).

Peter Scazzero, who has written *Emotionally Healthy Spirituality*,[15] is a man who has recognised that we cannot be spiritually mature unless we are emotionally mature. I encourage all to read his book (I only wish we had been his publisher!).

Social Needs

As we have already discussed, we are not able to fully live or function on our own; we need other people. We are social beings and we need a balance of being with others and being alone.

I have recently found a barre fitness class,[16] which has been great for my physical needs and also good socially. The instructor has made it fun, leading with chat and challenging us, and we have been able to get to know one another a bit more. She has also taken videos from time to time and circulated them to us. This has encouraged us to feel a sense of belonging in the group, and it increases our feeling of security.

My church has been a place of safety and peace for me too. I feel I belong there and am among good, safe people. During the lockdown we were able to access church online. It wasn't the same, but it was still there for us, and we were able to look forward to being together again in the future.

---

[15] Peter Scazzero, *Emotional Healthy Spirituality* (Zondervan, 2017 – updated).

[16] Barre fitness combines ballet-inspired moves with Pilates, dance, yoga and strength training. Most classes use a ballet barre and classic dance moves.

What an amazing feeling, when we can embrace once again things that have been withheld from us.

Community come together through a world crisis is something I thought I would never see. The world is often on the edge or right in the middle of a drama, and during the coronavirus pandemic every person was affected. It was heart-warming to see people help their neighbours in ways that many haven't seen since war times. I am thrilled that the community could adapt and become what we are meant to be for one another in times of crisis.

Walking one day during the lockdown, I met a man with his dog. He was walking with a crutch and I got the feeling he was on his own in life. I realised I may be the only person he would speak to that day, so I engaged with him, and as I left, he said,
    'What a lovely day to sit in the sun and read a book.'

I wanted to say,
    'I'm currently writing a book to encourage people to do that!'

But instead I said to him,
    'Yes it is, and I hope you get to enjoy that. However, some of us have to work today.' I told him I was I was heading home to meet counselling clients online.

'Well, I thank you for doing that, for being there to help us all, for being on the frontline at this time.'

I was totally choked up as I had not seen myself as that. To be thanked by someone I've never counselled, for helping others, is so at the heart of my being. This gentleman knew the ripple effect and was so thankful, so sincere, it was heart-warming.

This changed my day and my thinking – that small gesture created a huge ripple for me.

Crystal Clear: When We Are Out of Balance

I had a moment when my lovely crystal ring shot its precious gem across the room, having got caught on the microwave door. I felt sad and disappointed to start with. Then my attention was drawn to the fact that one corner of the ring was damaged, which meant it could no longer hold the gem in place. One of the four corners being bent out of place meant that all balance was lost, and the grip of the setting was no longer strong.

This made me think about how life can be. Emotionally exhausted, we can lose the determination to get to the gym or shop for good food. Then we may start to eat badly and feel a bit lower, so we then don't have the energy to exercise. We start to feel demoralised and our spiritual strength then goes down too. We can dip pretty easily, even those with true grit.

Realising what is going on is a big step forward. We need to recognise that we are under strain emotionally, practically or in any area.

- ► Take time to take time – even when we are not forced to anymore!
- ► Stop and reflect to see what is going on.
- ► That check-up we do on our car, our computer, our friends and our family, why not do it on ourselves?
- ► Take time to mend, heal and return to our true, fully functioning selves.

Allowing our true colours to shine through is surely the ideal life state we should be in. Rather than staying in the difficult places, repeating the same cycle or pattern, it's much healthier to dig a bit deeper to see what happened to tip us over.

One story brought home to me how hard it was to carry on when one member of a family falls down. Like the ring, one edge was weak, so the sparkle fell out.

My husband fell into a painful and repeated pattern of drinking and becoming aggressive. He was our rock, our provider, my children's father, my lover and my best friend. Then he became our aggressor, our enemy, taking from us instead of providing. It all fell apart. There was no balance. I tried to be mother, provider and to keep the family together. Through pain, vulnerability, anger and despair I tried to be both Mum and Dad; I tried to be everything to fill the gap, but I soon realised I could not be both.

Fighting to keep our home and feed us was a daily battle. The person who had been my confidant had now become the source of pain and conflict. How easily it seemed to break when we were caught off guard. Even though I had sensed there was something wrong many times and had tried to address it, there was no honesty or openness from my husband. Eventually the day came when it fell apart.

This could not be fixed; it was damaged forever because, without honesty, there was nowhere to go.

Somewhere, the unconditional love we had pledged to each other had gone, and all that was left was a battle.

Sadly, this led to divorce. This was something I had not foreseen happening in my life.

Honesty is vital to keep a relationship healthy and strong, as is allowing the other to act upon the changes needed and to keep talking to each other.

Labelled 'Divorced'

I have had to learn to see myself as the person I am today, rather than as an ex-wife, divorced, single. To begin with, it was a label I was fighting not to have: 'divorced'. I fought it for as long as I could. The label or the new box I had to tick hit me in the heart each time. 'Ms' was not a title I had ever expected to have. I had to let the pain come and I had to feel it to move on from it.

Now I am happy with who I am; I am happy inside and I know myself better. I am not a label of a failed marriage. I did not fail; I worked at it, but it takes two, and if he was not working at it I had to let it go. I had to move forward into a new life I could create for myself. Simply said, although not simply done.

This takes a lot of true grit and patience with yourself and with others. Others will want to pigeonhole you, label you and limit you; some won't be there to help you when you need it the most, or they will try to control you. Yet there will also be genuine people willing you on to a better time in your life.

Grab hold of yourself, grab hold of them and go for it. Life will get better, and the ring image of security on all corners can return. Even if you are on your own, you can live from the strength that is within you already. Can we have unconditional love for ourselves?

The Pink Lady

Unconditional love leads me to mention the wonderful romantic novelist Barbara Cartland. My mum became a friend of hers and went to visit her. She told me how amazing it was to sit with her and chat in her very pink house!

Barbara wore it and lived with it all around: pink, a colour that to me represents unconditional love.

But I do wonder what her background was. For me, this looks like a strong pattern that screams out a need for unconditional love. Of course, we all have this need, but it is not as obvious as it was in this vibrant and colourful lady who shone her colours out in her books. The lover of romance and the lover of love. When she passed away, I hope she felt that love in her heart.

Let's Sing Our True Colours

You may have guessed that one of my all-time favourite songs is
   'True Colours', sung by Cyndi Lauper. It resonated with me in my youth, and now, as a trained professional adult, it's still the same. But now I know why. I love to truly be myself, and I feel able to shine, unlike that shy and nervous girl hiding behind my brothers.

Yet I can still find out more things about myself, what I enjoy, and give new things a go. I can feast on life and go for the next phase.

I was chatting to a counselling friend recently, who said,

'They say that if I go as far as I can go, to the end of my current line, then I'll be able to see my next step. Doors will open to me, but only if I have already done all I can myself. I will not be left without a new track.' Wonderful, scary and a huge step of faith! That's when you discover that your true colours are beautiful like a rainbow – I hope!

Retreat to Advance

I mentioned earlier that, during my mentoring with Rachel Elnaugh, I spoke out my dream of running retreats. Unbeknown to me, I would have the opportunity to step out on to this path. I had spoken it out and it was heard and received, and then it came back to me.

At a business club dinner I met a great guy called Ian Harvey, who heard me talk about my dream and invited me to his place in France. The following year, Sarah Grace Retreats happened, with Michele Guinness very kindly being with us.

Journeying with authors also led to wanting to run my own writers' retreats, and this started to happen too. This was a dream I had held even before I started working in publishing. Originally I wanted to offer retreats to leaders, to give them respite, and this then led to offering writers' retreats too.

We offer time out for each person, whether a leader, writer, volunteer, retiree, mother, father, young person, ex-boarder, abused . . . I could go on. We enable them to find their true flavour and passions.

Stepping out, or should I say swimming, out of my depth to run this retreat had given me sleepless nights, excitement and butterflies in my stomach. I have had similar thoughts about the books I have published! I have had many sinking, negative thoughts of,

'What if this is just a good idea of mine that wasn't really meant to happen?'

'What if they don't enjoy it?'

'What if they know more than I do?'

So the fear kicked in, first as a thought, and then the feelings hurried back, with adrenaline rushing around. Then I was thankful for the detox app that I could follow daily on my phone. I went back to my narrative and worked on turning it around from:

'I am on my own, I won't manage this' to:

'I can succeed, as God is with me.'

True Flavour

It is a gift for me to bring the flavour out of each person where I have the opportunity.

I was making a cup of tea one day and really squeezing the bag.

'That's what you do, Sarah,' Malcolm said to me.

'What, squeeze as much into life as possible?'

(This can be viewed as a good or a bad thing, I guess.)

'No, you bring out the flavour to make it the best it can be.'

Maybe I should have called this chapter 'True Flavour'!

Going In Deep

I love to swim, and each place I visit I seek out a pool. I am not a great swimmer; I just love the feeling of being in the water, enjoying a quiet moment of calm. If it's busy, I hold back until it's quiet, to enjoy that moment of breaking into the water and creating my own ripple. I love the feeling of weightlessness and freedom from everything but the thoughts floating around in my head. I try to use the skills I have gained to captivate each thought and slow my mind down.

I have found other ways of unwinding and seeking that peaceful place, such as walking, especially out in the sunshine. I like to seek culturally vibrant places to start the creative process, and then a quiet place to sit for a while and write. This helps me move into the right place to prepare and to create, whether I am working on a book cover or another piece that I need to work on, or just to clear my mind to be able to see clients.

I found a great pool in Lanzarote – apparently, it's the best one on the island. Now I feel I must check them all out to see whether it's true! It's a shaped, heated outdoor pool. I swam around it in the sunshine, I had it all to myself. Then I changed direction and started to swim across it.

Then I suddenly started to feel fearful: the risk of being in the centre, and was I swimming too soon after my breakfast? What if I sink? Then in the moment I recognised the analogy of how we can stay stuck or we can step out into the unknown, into the deep, feeling suddenly vulnerable.

People were sitting and lying by the pool. In that moment I forgot every single one, as I felt alone. Then, to the other extreme, a moment later I thought of the embarrassment I would experience if I were actually to sink! This was followed by a response in my spirit rather than in my head:

'OK, so I can pray. God is with me.'

'I am here with you.' This was the detox thought I had been working on.

Then I became aware of the lifeguard having only me on his watch at that time.

This process of analysing took place without anyone having any idea it was happening. It took only seconds, as I was still in the central, deep waters of the loveliest pool in Lanzarote. I kept swimming, and considered how we go through these thoughts constantly in our lives. Leaving these thoughts unchecked can be paralysing, deflecting our gifting and strapping us down.

I have an image of Gulliver, from the book *Gulliver's Travels* by Jonathan Swift, being held down by small ropes. I may have seen this in a film: lots of tiny little ropes, secured with pegs into the ground. These ropes can be like our mental processes: so powerful, so silent to the outside world, and yet they affect us and everyone around us.

I broke through something in that moment in the pool. As I swam on, I realised it was a deep fear from childhood of dark, deep water, as I couldn't see what was in there. I was terrified of it, although I had actually learnt to swim on the banks of this water where it was clearer. I guess I had a fear of taking a few strokes and being in too deep, fearing being swallowed up.

That was a real fear as I saw the deep water in front of me and would quickly doggy-paddle back to the side. In the here and now, in that clear pool, I focused in on the moment. It became freeing and a significant moment of release, like letting go of something that had chained me down. I knew God was there, but everyone else disappeared to me in that connecting moment, and I enjoyed it immensely.

To all onlookers, who had vanished from my mind in that moment, nothing was different from the rest of my swim. However, it was like I had taken a skydive, it was so exhilarating.

When I was young I had too many moments of being pushed out of my comfort zone by my adventurous brothers, so my tendency was to either throw myself straight in or quickly retreat. This was a moment I allowed myself to have. How wonderful and powerful to find it for myself.

Penny-dropping Moments

I do love a penny-dropping moment in the counselling room – being with a client and helping them find a key to something deep within. I have been in therapy myself and know the moment: it really is like something falling into place. That penny-dropping moment cannot be done *to* you; it has to be found *by* you, although others can help you to find it.

We are all on a journey, and as we travel within ourselves, each great moment we quietly have is a celebration for the world too. Every time we face our fears and step out, we become just a little bit nearer to being whole.

Time to Celebrate

Celebrating can be overrated . . . er, no!

I feel we should definitely be celebrating more.

I have many clients who find it difficult to celebrate good things as the emphasis is on what has gone wrong. I am not necessarily talking about birthdays, weddings and so on, as marketing and media have that covered well and we are doing that more and more. There is emphasis now on events such as baby showers, week-long hen and stag dos, prom nights with limos and so on.

I am talking about celebrating our smaller life experiences and those things that are hidden. I admire the way the Jewish community celebrates the coming of age. This gives a rite of passage into adulthood, which is significant. I remember encouraging my husband to take my daughter out to celebrate when she started her periods. This was to celebrate womanhood. Celebrating our bodies can be done daily – appreciating and celebrating each other. Such gestures are easy to make and easily missed.

Celebrating can be as small as an acknowledgement, a moment of expression, not necessarily pulling out the champagne. (However, I hope I will be doing this when I receive feedback on this book from you!) I try to take a moment of liking something or observing something and telling the person there and then if I can, otherwise the moment gets lost.

Sadly, we are hearing and reading more about emotional distress and harming our bodies. How can we turn this around?

Motivation: Was Bob Blessed or Robbed?

Meet Bob. Bob does not need to work as he was given a house when he was twenty years old. In his mid-thirties, his life falls apart, and he can't work out what is wrong with him. He cannot seem to feel the right feelings towards his wife.

He loves his children but has to leave the marriage. He is unable to hold anger.

We discover together that Bob's father could not show anger, so Bob doesn't know how to express it himself. In learning this, he starts to allow himself to feel, and comes off drugs and drink. He starts to express the anger outwardly rather than self-harming with drugs. He starts to see how lack of motivation from being given a house has affected his life. Fortunately, he has been able to recognise this soon enough to see the damage before travelling on into his future and creating a further ripple of drama and discontent.

Our lives are in our hands. But how do we do life when we don't know who we are? We look for completion in a relationship with another, and we look for them to complete us. I remember telling my husband that he completed me, and it felt really good – until I realised that he never said it back. Now that did not feel at all complete.

I had to go through the eye of the needle to find myself and who I was, having come out of a twenty-year marriage. People would say,

'Now it's your time to do what you want,' as if I had been set free like a butterfly. Yet with no time to process the change, and just being thrown into a new phase, it was terrifying. I thought I knew who I was: a wife and a mother. Then I became single and my children were less in need of me. Now who was I?

I recall being told,
    'They will soon be off your hands and so you'll be fine,' as if my children were some kind of burden to me physically and financially rather than my source of love and joy and my purpose for the last seventeen years.

So I went on a search to find who I used to be before my marriage and children. I discovered that I had changed and grown, but I still wasn't sure into what or whom. My identity was being torn away moment by moment. Yesterday I was a loving wife and mother of two; today my thoughts were,
    'You are on your own and no one is there for you; you're of no value to anyone anymore.'

Yet I was being told,
    'Now run with the dreams and desires that you actually didn't know you had. Go on, soar on that little flight!'

I felt I was going to crash and burn in many pieces. It was only because of my lovely children, my faith in God and my family and friends that I survived. I found the strength to find myself again. I was different from the girl who had married the man of her dreams. Now, as a woman, a mother of two and a Christian, I had new dreams.

Carpool Karaoke

A dream or a mad idea, I'm not sure, but either way it was a blast of a day being in a car with Mal Corden (James Corden's dad) and The Sons of Pitches. We chose the song 'More Than Gold', which was written by them, because of the words,

'Loving everything that is thrown at your feet'.

With my dyslexic nature, I thought outside the box and made this event happen. You can see the final outcome on YouTube.[17]

Something that makes your heart sing will come through when you are more comfortable in your own skin. We did this together, collaborating together, each of us using our gifts and not being threatened by each other. I truly found like-minded people who share my values and celebrate the good.

The Sons of Pitches are an awesome group of young lads who met at the University of Birmingham. In a brilliant bit of collaboration, they blended their fine voices to win a national competition before finishing their degrees.

More than Gold

When you're focused on a purpose and a reason
And it's all you live and breathe
Yes I know, it takes a little less you see
I know it's hard to find the focus and the time
When you're living so carefree
But I know, it's easier for me

---

[17] 'Mal Corden Carpool Karaoke – The Sons of Pitches', 27 December 2018, https://www.youtube.com/watch?v=vMvgpNKHwG4 (accessed 11 February 2020).

Love everything that is thrown at your feet
Try it sometime and I think you'll agree

Cause I'm hoping for more than gold
Have you got it in you?
Reaching for every goal
Yeah, you've got it
Hoping for more than gold
Have you got it in you?
Reaching for every goal
Yeah, you've got it

It's not about the silver or the gold
    or the image you display
It's the path you take on the way
When you're lacking any motivation
    every single day
You should know, I've got some words to say

Love everything that is thrown at your feet
Learn over time and I think you'll agree

I got a single purpose but for you it might be hard
Just picking up your feet and getting off the sofa
I got the mindset, I got the magic beans
You gotta face your giant and
    then chop down the tree
Inspiration, motivation – nothing
    more than words
So drop the dictionary and just
    keep up the search
You the golden girl, I got the silver,
But like diamonds we will be stronger.

Cause I'm hoping for more than
   gold [you the golden girl]
Have you got it in you?
Reaching for every goal
Yeah, you've got it
Hoping for more than gold [you the golden girl]
Have you got it in you?
Reaching for every goal
Yeah, you've got it.[18]

---

[18] The Sons of Pitches, 'More than Gold', (2017). Used with permission.

Gracelets

A wonderful little gem for us to look towards: make now the best time you can have.

What might that look like – truly living, and not just surviving? To make a difference, to be real, to cultivate an environment for us all to flourish. A better you is better for me!

By seeing each other's strengths and building each other up, we could create a better world around us.

Our mental processes are so powerful, so silent to the outside world, yet they affect us and everyone else around us.

Contentment on the inside can create this as it ripples out to others, as they want what we have. Then, standing side by side, interlocking, makes a difference to all our lives and the Kingdom – be it the United Kingdom or God's Kingdom, we all benefit.

Celebrating our bodies can be done daily, as we appreciate and celebrate each other. These moments are easy to make and easily missed. We read more about harming our bodies and emotional distress. How can we turn this around?

We are more than gold – so very much more!

Your Ripple

So, like Barbara Cartland, does your colour shine out?

Does your need for love or your need for something shine in a way that all can see but you haven't seen it yet?
What could you change to really live and not just survive? What difference would that make to others around you?

What can you reach for that, like The Sons of Pitches, is more than gold? 'Have you got it in you' to change and make a difference?

Chapter 10

A Contagious Ripple

A Creative, Gentle Ripple

As my mum would tell me,
   'Sarah, nothing lasts forever, all good things have to
come to an end.' *Journey with Grace* has been a life-
changing experience for me and I hope for you as we have
journeyed together.

I gave everything my best shot, taking care of things so they
would last. My friends have admired the way I have managed
to keep things functioning well all this time. Somewhere on
my journey this made me feel more secure and in control, I
guess, but keeping hold of something also gave me pleasure.
When I lost something, it would drive me nuts trying to
find it. It would be hard to let go and I would go around and
around, how could I have done it differently or if I could still
retrieve it.

I always do things to the best of my ability, despite my
challenges. Making this book the best it can be has been an
incredible journey every day over many, many months. Some
days it feels rather like a tsunami. Then I try to bring it back
to a gentle ripple of peace, reminding myself that today
I can only achieve so much, and I am still on my journey
as I write.

Endings and Time to Fly . . .

As all good things – and all things, actually – do come to an end, we should really hold this as a thought, not as something negative, but as a fact. When I know that the time I have with a client is limited for some reason – perhaps they are going on a long trip so we will have a break – it changes the therapy. A time limit can be something positive to focus the mind.

We do not know how long we have here on Earth, yet so often we act as though we have forever. If we knew how long we had, what would we do?

Would we do things differently?

Would it make us grow small, or twice as tall?

If we had known the coronavirus pandemic and the subsequent lockdown were coming, would we have done anything differently?

A fellow student from my postgraduate days was also a young mum. She was loved for being 'Mum', for being there and being so lovely to everyone. She would shoot off as quickly as possible to get back to her children and when we had weekend workshops her children would visit during her downtime. She was always there for them. We met when she was battling with bowel cancer and she said,
'You know me, Sarah, I never wanted to do anger, I pushed it down. That became normal, so did bleeding from time to time, I ignored it'.

We had a moment of sadness looking at each other without words but a sense of wondering if this was why; was she holding that anger in her stomach? Was it too late or would she survive it?

She put her hand on her stomach and we had a hug.

Tragically, the following year she died at the age of thirty-seven, leaving her two young children, one of whom had leukaemia. We were all so shocked and upset for her family, and we knew how heartbroken she would have been at leaving them.

Looking for comfort I went for a swim, seeking complete peace and calm. I realised as I allowed the waters to settle, the surface glistened beautifully as the sunshine reflected on it and also the ceiling above . . . I just breathed. Realising that even my breath made a ripple . . . I watched it gently move the water before me. My breath changing the world around me. Knowing my friend had just died, no more, no breath. Her life done, rippling out pain of her going. Her infectious laugh and vibrancy gone, a ripple of sadness as she breathes no more.

It took me weeks to come to terms with it. I hadn't been present in her everyday life, yet knowing the impact of her going caused me pain. I realised as I swam that while we still breathe we are creating a ripple, even if we are not doing anything . . . we are still 'here', which creates something. Just by being here, we are affecting other people.

Then I stood completely still in the pool: no ripples; it was completely flat. It made me realise that even when we are not here anymore, no longer able to engage or connect, the ripple goes on for the ones we have touched.

This is true for anyone who has lost someone; the ripple of their existence goes on and on. Yet perhaps we ourselves feel that we might be forgotten, while we are still here and when we are gone. Sometimes the ripple is stronger in our absence; often we miss those who are not at the party more than we appreciate those who are there.

So I consider the value of my life: do I value it is as much as others value me? Do I really know how valued I am? Then in an instant I can lose it. My wish is for each of us to really know our value and worth. The moment we are not breathing, no longer a living change to change the ripple we make, yet whilst we are here we have a chance. Our value and worth reflected on, examined, thought over longingly and missed. Guilt may come and memories flood back. Why didn't I call or message when I thought of them, that social I was going to plan to see her, that book I wanted to tell her about and that time we could have had . . . gone.

I wonder if we can live today like we value ourselves and others as if it were only today we have. The cliché of living like it's our last and only day.

So my mum's words repeating in my head,
   'Things don't last forever, Sarah.'

I had no idea why she would say this so often, but it felt bad until I hit difficult times, 'thank God they don't last forever' I thought and realised the flip side of her wise words.
   Let's use today to gain and gleam what we can but also tell others what they mean to us even if it's a small memory to share, it could change their ripple and yours.

If there is one other gem I would share with you, that my mum taught me, it would be this: do not save things for best, use them now. She told me how her family kept their front room beautifully laid out just in case the Queen came to visit. They lived in Ashford, Middlesex, so not too far from London, but it was still highly unlikely she would pop in. This meant they never enjoyed the good stuff – it was kept well and ready, but not for them to use or share.

I endeavour to use my best most days and pray that there will be more. I have learnt to enjoy it now. We can take that into relationships as well: enjoy them now.

We need to give ourselves time to change our patterns of being, and allow others to do the same. There is a blessing in giving others the chance to change, rather than putting them into a box or labelling them. Our fixed opinion can keep others fixed in our minds. Does it mean they can't change? Can you change?

March of the Penguins

I started to think again about 'partner' and 'parents' as I reflected how my son loved penguins when he was a young boy. Josh loved penguins so much he had nine imaginary penguin friends who went to nursery with him. They were quite a lot to handle, as we all got into the car with my daughter in a carry seat! I would go to shut the front door to hear his little voice pipe up,
    'Mummy, they are not all out yet.'

'Oh! Sorry, Josh,' and I would start counting them out of the door with him!

Gorgeous and fun, these little imaginary friends led to many images of mum, dad and baby penguins. We watched the *March of the Penguins* documentary together and the film *Happy Feet!*

Penguins live in close families, dedicating themselves to each other and their young. How right it can feel, what contentment we find within, when it goes well and the family thrives. This is what we miss and ache for when it is incomplete. Even if it has never been known, we still miss it, as we are wired to love and to be loved. Being loved leads to feeling loveable and being able to love. The full package should be expected and desired.

A Jig

During one of the moments when I was considering being loved, I saw an image of a jig. I used to play for many hours in the back of my stepdad's van, and used lots of carpentry tools. I thought about the jig as a stabiliser, holding the wood in place. I could see the link – we can be a jig to others, and this can shift as they become that for us, depending on our needs at the time. This can create a partnership rather than dependence. It is another measure of the unconditional love we all desire.

Intimacy Broken

A client shared her story with me as we explored intimacy and what it meant to her:
'I find myself connecting together how the intimacy of God, my brokenness of intimacy by my father, can be restored.'

She continued,

'Being kissed by my partner as he lay next to me suddenly took me back, for some reason, to my stepfather kissing me. I didn't like it and withdrew. It felt wrong, upsetting, and I knew it was so deep I couldn't put it into words. How do I tell him how I feel without upsetting him? I would deliberately never go out with guys older than me to avoid looking for father figures.'

'Your partner is older than you?' I enquired.

'Yes, he's older than me. Is it that? We've been seeing each other for a year, so surely it would have happened before now?'

'What do you think changed? Was something else happening at the time?'

'Actually, now you say that, yes. Someone had suggested we were wrong to be intimate without being married.'

'Was it that? Did it suddenly feel wrong to lie together? Kissing is intimate and explorative – was this wrong?'

Whatever the answer to that, the comment had hit a nerve, a memory, a pain and the intimacy had been stolen from her. Early in her life her innocence and trust were broken by her stepfather.

'Am I no longer free to be in a relationship with any man I may be vulnerable with? That kiss of betrayal, that level of intimacy in a wrong relationship I felt deep in my chest, in my heart. Now it has reappeared.'

'I sense such pain as a result of the betrayal by someone who should have been caring for you, such a deep pain within you.'

Tears were flowing and I sensed that the deep pain that was being reached had been buried. As hard as it was, that pain needed to be brought to the surface and be seen, heard and felt. It had never been expressed or verbalised before.

The following week she came back, bursting to share what had happened. 'I have had a lump on my chest, near my heart. It's only small but it's itchy. I scratched off the top earlier in the week and suddenly it started bleeding. I was aware it was sore but hadn't realised it was bleeding so much. I looked down to see what looked like a shot wound, with a splatter of blood coming out from the centre, almost like a bullet had gone in. Later, when I was praying, I could see the shot mark in my chest like a bullet into my heart. It was small but direct – a clear shot! I saw it so clearly and I really wanted to sob.

'At church last week, the talk was about light and thanking God for the light shining in the darkness,' she continued. 'I could see the light being shone into this area as my heart was healing from the pain that had been hidden in there for a while. What a relief it has all been to get it out.'

'I am wondering if it is like the lump being brought to the surface and removed.'

'Yes, exactly that, and it's completely healed up!

I now want to kiss my partner in moments of intimacy without a shadow over me pulling away the loveliness of its intent.

'Occasionally I still feel my heart is fragile.'

'It sounds like you are learning from it rather than pulling the shutters back down.'

'By God's grace I will manage to be fully loved again, I'm sure of that.'

That story is how a contagious ripple can be good or bad. With awareness, we can turn even bad ripples into good.

During my training, my peers saw how much I was going through – it was an extremely difficult time. They told me at the end,
   'Even if we wanted to give up, we couldn't. We saw you were going through so much but you wouldn't give up, so how could we?'

I didn't see it at the time, but I was sticking with it as I did not want my children to give up, so how could I?

That's the kind of ripple we can be proud of!

Regifted Years

Truly celebrating who we are and our gifts, not competing, being able to walk alongside someone and encourage them to be the best they can be:

what better gift of being alive and being able to really bring someone else alive?!

Consider the retirement years of our lives. I would love to create a new name for these years, perhaps 'regifted' or 'precious years'. Obviously, retirement is time to relax, to enjoy less pressure and to live out the dreams we have not yet lived. Hopefully it is a time when there is still energy, some financial security, wisdom to regift and encourage others following us in their own journeys. Lessons can be passed on and learnt from.

We do not need to wait until we retire to create such a generous ripple!

If we are able to do it, why not do it now?

Enjoy seeing others grow around you, and we may find we can grow too.

Courgettes, Not Marrows

In a session with a client, we were exploring how she was managing her health, her time and her relationships during her retirement. An analogy came freely as she shared about her pleasure from her garden. It was important to her to take time to attend to her courgettes before they became marrows. Courgettes are manageable, tasty and small enough to enjoy. Left to their own devices, they grow into marrows. I asked her what these are like for her.

'They are large, dirty, hard to deal with, cumbersome, taste strange and can be hard to get rid of. They feel heavy and

I can't do much with them. They get dumped on the side; they're dirty and hard to manage.'
Emotions that are not kept in check, even though they are pushed down, will continue to grow, like a marrow. At some point they will need to be dealt with. We could see the link with her emotional well-being.

Don't we all want courgettes instead of marrows? Then we can re-gift courgettes to others around us rather than leaving behind heavy loads that need clearing away.

Finding Our Way to Grace

This book would not be complete without mentioning grace in its fullness.

What is it, and what keeps us from finding it?

What is keeping us away from our dreams, desires and plans for our lives?

Discouragement and rejection are among the most powerful tools. They work to prevent us from feeling content and stop us pushing on towards our goals. Top this off with a few more layers of feelings of failure and failed relationships, and our course can be set in the wrong direction. Pulling it back is like steering a ship in a different direction. Jealousy and self-esteem issues can pop up at any time as we see others doing well and staying with their relationships and on their journey.

To start turning that ship around, we need to make and be able to see small changes, no matter how small.

The small changes will lead to bigger changes, and eventually that ship will turn in the right direction. Keeping ourselves looking at the positives and growing the hope in our hearts, as this helps us gain an inner strength of belief.

For me, one of these positives is to play music, especially worship songs that are uplifting and help me to build my relationship with God. I feel loved and then I can share that love. This makes complete sense to me – we cannot give out what we do not have. I rely on God's grace in my life more than anything else; I have had to learn to during the rocky times in life, now I enjoy it freely, daily.

God gives us grace unconditionally. We cannot earn it; grace is readily available to us whether we are a believer or not yet.
    What a gift I was missing before I believed.

I was really inspired by a sermon Mark Helvadjian from my church gave on God's grace. These are the points I picked up:

- ► We are called by name. God looks past our issues, problems and mistakes; he just sees us. That's grace.
- ► Grace enables fellowship with God; his door is always open.
- ► Grace humbles us in the areas of our life that need changing.
- ► Grace causes us to take note; it challenges us.
- ► Grace reveals God, his goodness and his mercy, making it possible for us to change.
- ► The fruit of grace enables us to overcome our circumstances. We will start to see him act in our lives when we look for the fruit.

- Grace causes good works: we cannot stay the same.
- Grace affirms us, shines on us and spurs us on.
- Grace is actively seeking us out – we cannot earn it.

I believe that God loves us too much to leave us the same; he wants us to grow and enjoy the very best, as every good dad does. This leaves me feeling loved, loveable and lovely, which means I am able to love and be loved.

Impactful Ripple

During the Second World War, Sir Nicholas Winton loved many children who became thankful to him for their lives: 669 Jewish children to be exact. Today 100,000 people's lives may have been affected through those he saved from the prison camps. Their lives are giving lives, as the generations go on, the ripple effect is still going on.

We might think,
   'I am only one person – how can I make a difference? Who am I to think I can help?'

What a privilege to see the ripple effect from the actions of this one man.

What if we could see the ripple effect of our actions, whether in business or our personal life, on those we have affected, including those we haven't even met but somehow we have had an effect on. Maybe we will meet them in heaven – what a privilege that would be!

To see the true effect of our ripple we need to find our passion and our calling. How wonderful when we find it and it flows.

When we find our true passion, it doesn't feel like work because it's a pleasure. However, your boss and others will see how you soar!

As our ripple stretches out over the years, we may not know who we touch and how. We are blessed if, like Doug Murrey mentioned earlier, we get to hear about it. But I believe it is best if we just get on with what is in our hearts, and if we see the ripple come back we are doubly blessed.

Knowing Your Worth

Let us stop regularly to appreciate each God-given moment. Let's stop and wait to see what he is saying to us. This can be hard to do as we seem to have things to plan for and work towards, but it is vital to find that balance of living in the moment and living life to the full.

Many good books and films contain both tears and laughter. Perhaps in this book I have jumped from some hard stories to some more light-hearted anecdotes to demonstrate my points. I hope you have managed to engage with each story along the way.

To end on a sad note is not my plan, but there is something I need to share now or my heart will burst.

As I write, the wildlife in Australia is being ravaged because of bush fires. All who know me know my love of Australia. In the inner sanctum of my bedroom I have a collection I call my koala sanctuary. Each collectable koala has its own story. Let me introduce them:

'Colney' lived on my mother's dressing table when I was a small child, and it was Colney who started my love of these cute animals. We lived in Colney Heath, hence his name. Colney is made of beautifully soft fur. He was sent to Mum from New South Wales in Australia by a family friend when I was a baby. I would sit and stroke him while she got ready to go out. He was like a comfort for me when she was out, but he never moved from her dressing table until she gave him to me one day. Colney is very special to me. His head is in danger of falling off, so he's safe in the sanctuary of my room.

'Hugs' I sent to my mum as a birthday gift from my trip in my twenties. He has arms that wrap around and stick together, so I was sending her a virtual hug!

Syd' was from Sydney (obviously!). He was my first big koala from my trip around the world. He's soft and huggable and from my favourite city in the world. Love him!

'Pauly' grabs at my heart. I took a trip to Australia to see my family for Christmas one year. My friend Paul was not expected to live for long. He also loved Australia, and my heart ached as I knew he would not get to see it again. I was his eyes and legs as I shared all I could with him on this trip. He asked me to bring him back a koala, so I bought a matching pair from a shop near the Opera House. To all our amazement, Paul was still with us when I returned home. He loved his gift and requested it to be in his coffin. I have mine, knowing he has his. Tears flow as I recall his smile when I entered his room with our twin koalas!

'Moneybags' is a koala money box to save up for my next trip to Australia – until I realised that even when it was full I had hundreds of pounds still to save! Moneybags is covered in cute, baggy lines and is stuffed to the brim with coins!

'Little Nellie' came home with me from another trip further up the coast near Avoca Beach, where the fires did not reach, thankfully. Nellie is small, compact and lifelike. Adorable! She is exactly like a koala I saw sitting in a tree once – it was such thrill to see an animal in its natural habitat. It seemed to be enjoying life, just as we should be. I have learnt a lot from animals over the years.

I tell you about my collection because koalas caught my heart years ago. I wanted a real koala sanctuary until I realised how many acres they need.

Now, as we see them possibly in danger of extinction, we are all suddenly aware of them.

Everywhere we went for a time despite being thousands of miles away they were of interest to us here in the UK: koala socks, soap, you name it. They were on our radar because they pull on our heart; they were being killed off and there was nothing we could do to stop the fires.

I have heard that one of the ladies who works on our Australian children's book series, *The Lost Sheep*, lost her dad in the fires. We can so easily forget about those who were helping the animals and those who were trying to protect their homes.

The only positive thing I can draw from these horrific fires in Australia that burnt as I wrote this is the compassion and community they created across the world. People were pulling together to fight a battle, to help the innocent and hurting. As mentioned earlier in relation to the coronavirus lockdown, community is being created from a crisis as we demonstrate how we all need each other and the ripple spreads wider and deeper.

20/20 Vision

Disasters such as the Australian bush fires and the coronavirus pandemic concentrate our minds on what is important. Maybe this will sharpen us and allow us to act more without fear. Can we give our time, our money and our hearts to what tugs on them, or do we just close them off again?

Publishing this book during 2020 has felt so timely. I have had difficulties with my eyes, so it's a dream for me to hear,
    'Sarah, you have 20/20 vision'!

I am hoping this book will give us all 20/20 vision of ourselves and our own lives and that this will allow us to see others around us in the same way. I long for us to have 20/20 vision of the world around us, to see it for what it is: its beauty, its pain and its brilliance.

We all like a good ending to a story, so I would like to share this last one with you:

Meet a Fully Functioning Human Being

Allow me to introduce you to Jake, a smart and intelligent twenty-year-old who turned his life around.

'I was happy with life, but I wanted more out of it.'

'So you wanted a more fulfilled life?' I asked.

'Yeah, I wanted a more fulfilled life! My biggest problem was that I wasn't motivated to do anything, so I didn't give myself a choice. I made myself change. I had an image of how I wanted to be which was different from how I was, so I guess I decided to make myself into that image.'

'So, Jake, you actually did have motivation, which was the image you desired. You had a revelation and you now seek it, since you have recognised what you want. Now it's bursting out of you! This is really you; the image you had was the real you. The shy guy playing video games endlessly was a limited version of you.'

'Yep, now I am unlimited! I could have stayed in my comfort zone, but I've lost weight, gained a girlfriend, have lots of friends at university and run the Cyber Society. I still don't know myself totally, but I am really keen to find out more about myself!'

'How exciting, Jake! Many people never do this, yet you're doing this at twenty. You have an immeasurably more exciting future than you did a year ago. I'm so proud of you!'

'We all are!' That's a chorus from Jake's mum, dad, sister, nanny, grandad and friends. That is why I had to share this! We all celebrate Jake's contagious ripple and we will all benefit from it, whether we realise it or not.

This is a wonderful story, and as I write it the song 'Immeasurably More' by Rend Collective starts to randomly played on my phone: this is hopefully for us all, including Jake!

Gracelets

Fully living free on the inside of ourselves, with 20/20 vision, can empower others to do the same. We can inspire beyond words if we allow it for ourselves first. Take a moment to think about how you feel. Are you excited about life and looking forward to sharing your story with others?

Allow yourself the privilege of fully living.

God, you see me and value me, do I really know this deep down, do any of us?

If we knew how long we had on Earth, would we do things differently? Would it make us grow small or twice as tall?

Your Ripple

We have explored all the aspects of truly living, of living live to the full.

Are you able to give out courgettes or are you still producing marrows?

Regifting – are you in the 'precious years' and wanting to regift to others?

Your talents and gifts can help others. What could this look like? Do you need help to see what they are and how they could be helpful?

Are you ready and able to create a contagious and regifting ripple?
I am here to help . . . I would love to see and know your contagious ripple.

Further Reading

Pennie Aston, 'The Emotional Repercussions of Dyslexia', LinkedIn, 24 January 2016 (https://www.linkedin.com/pulse/emotional-repercussions-dyslexia-pennie-aston/, accessed 19 May 2020).

John Bowlby, *Attachment and Loss* (Pimlico, 1997).

John Bowlby, *The Making and Breaking of Affectional Bonds* (Routledge, 2005).

Jane Brocklehurst, 'Fear of Success', *Christian Writer* (Spring 2019).

Brené Brown, *Daring Greatly: How the Courage to Be Vulnerable Transforms the Way We Live, Love, Parent, and Lead* (Penguin, 2015).

Catherine Campbell, *Journey with Me* (IVP, 2018).

Andrew Davies, *Pressed But Not Crushed* (Malcolm Down Publishing, 2015).

Robert de Board, *Counselling for Toads: A Psychological Adventure* (Routledge, 1998).

Nick Duffell, *The Making of Them: The British Attitude to Children and the Boarding School System* (Lone Arrow Press, 2000).

Nick Duffell, *Wounded Leaders: British Elitism and the Entitlement Illusion – A Psychohistory* (Lone Arrow Press, 2014, 2015).

Nick Duffell and Thurstine Basset, *Trauma, Abandonment and Privilege: A Guide to Therapeutic Work with Boarding School Survivors* (Routledge, 2016).

Caris Grimes, *Failing Intelligently: Facing and Learning Through the Impact of Failure* (Sarah Grace Publishing, 2019).

Mark Helvadjian, sermon notes on Grace (2018).

Wendy H. Jones, *Motivation Matters: Revolutionise Your Writing One Creative Step at a Time* (2019).

Rob Joy, *Coming Out Gold: A Quest for Sexual Purity* (Malcolm Down Publishing, 2018).

Josephine Klein, *Our Need for Others and its Roots in Infancy* (Routledge, 1987).

Dr Caroline Leaf, *Switch On Your Brain: The Key to Peak Happiness, Thinking, and Health* (Baker Books, 2013).

Claire Musters, *Taking Off the Mask* (Authentic Media, 2017).

Emily Owen, *Still Emily* (Sarah Grace Publishing, 2016).

Patrick Reagan with Lisa Hoeksma, *Honesty Over Silence: It's OK Not To Be OK* (CWR, 2018).

Peter Scazzero, *Emotionally Healthy Spirituality: A 40-day Journey with the Daily Office* (Zondervan, 2008, 2014).

Joy Schaverien, *Boarding School Syndrome* (Routledge, 2015).

Mark Stibbe, *Home at Last: Freedom from Boarding School Pain* (Malcolm Down Publishing, 2016).

Mark and Cherith Stibbe, *Restoring the Fallen: Creating Safe Spaces For Those Who Fail* (Malcolm Down Publishing, 2019).

Martha Stark MD, *A Heart Shattered, The Private Self, and a Life Unlived*, available as a free download from the International Psychotherapy Institute: https://www.freepsychotherapybooks.org/ebook/a-heart-shattered-the-private-self-and-a-life-unlived/ (accessed 13 February 2020).

David Strutt, *Sanctuary: Moments in His Presence* (365-day devotional) (Malcolm Down Publishing, 2017).

Dr Henry Cloud and Dr John Townsend, *Boundaries* (Zondervan,1992).

Donald Winnicott, *Babies and Their Mothers* (Free Association Books, 1988).

Donald Winnicott, *Playing and Reality* (Routledge Classics, 2005).

Martin Young, *This Is That* (Malcolm Down Publishing, 2020).

Ruth Feldman PhD (see UCL notes for further ref. Simms-Mann professor of Developmental Neuroscience).

Other resources and websites

Klaus E. Krogh, Type Founder, 2K Typographic Design
https://www.2kdenmark.com/

Made by Dyslexia: http://madebydyslexia.org/

British Dyslexia Association: https://www.bdadyslexia.org.uk/

Dyslexia the Gift: https://www.dyslexia.com/

Torch Trust, providing resources for people with sight loss:
http://torchtrust.org/

Cameron Grant Memorial Trust: https://www.camgrant.org.uk/

Further Help

Author Coaching

Author coaching can look different for everyone, as it is so personal – rather like therapy. I hear the authors' ideas, dreams and desires. Often the coaching involves slowing the process down so each phase of writing is fully absorbed personally. At one point I even told an author (in front of Malcolm) that even if the book did not come out at the end, it was the journey that was important. It's about what God is teaching you and wanting you to share with the world as well as you enjoy the writing process. Malcolm nearly fell off his chair and went completely pale!

We have seen many manuscripts completely transformed through the coaching process. It has been a joy to see how God had linked my psychotherapy training with publishing – something I would never have expected.

Once the coaching starts and we have seen where we are going, I try to bring more flavour out of the story by looking at areas that might have been missed simply because the author is too close to their own story. My role is to gently encourage further exploration of the emotional depths.

Each author will go at their own pace and I listen to how they are finding their way. Sometimes this means encouraging them to tease out more emotions.

Counselling

If you feel there are areas of your life that you would benefit from exploring in a deeper way, I would recommend talking to a counsellor.

Association of Christian Counsellors (ACC)
www.acc-uk.org

British Association of Counsellors and Practitioners (BACP)
www.bacp.co.uk

Counselling Directory

Making Contact

If you would like to contact me with regards to exploring the possibility of counselling, please contact me adding Counselling to the subject line:

Contact: grace4counselling@gmail.com
www.sarahmgrace.co.uk

Sarah Grace
Psychotherapist/Counsellor
Post Graduate Diploma in Contemporary Therapeutic Counselling

Professional registered member of the British Association of Counsellors and Psychotherapists. (Reg. M.B.A.C.P)

Retreats

Please email me on sarah@sarahmgrace.co.uk and title your email 'Retreat'.

Please email to ask for specific requirements as these can be discussed and tailored to your requirements.

Additional Services from Sarah Grace

For further help please email me on sarah@sarahmgrace.co.uk and title your emails specifically:

Creative Therapy
Play Therapy
Dyslexic Business Advice
Dyslexic Personal Support

Journal
with Grace

HOME
at Last

FREEDOM FROM
BOARDING SCHOOL PAIN

MARK STIBBE

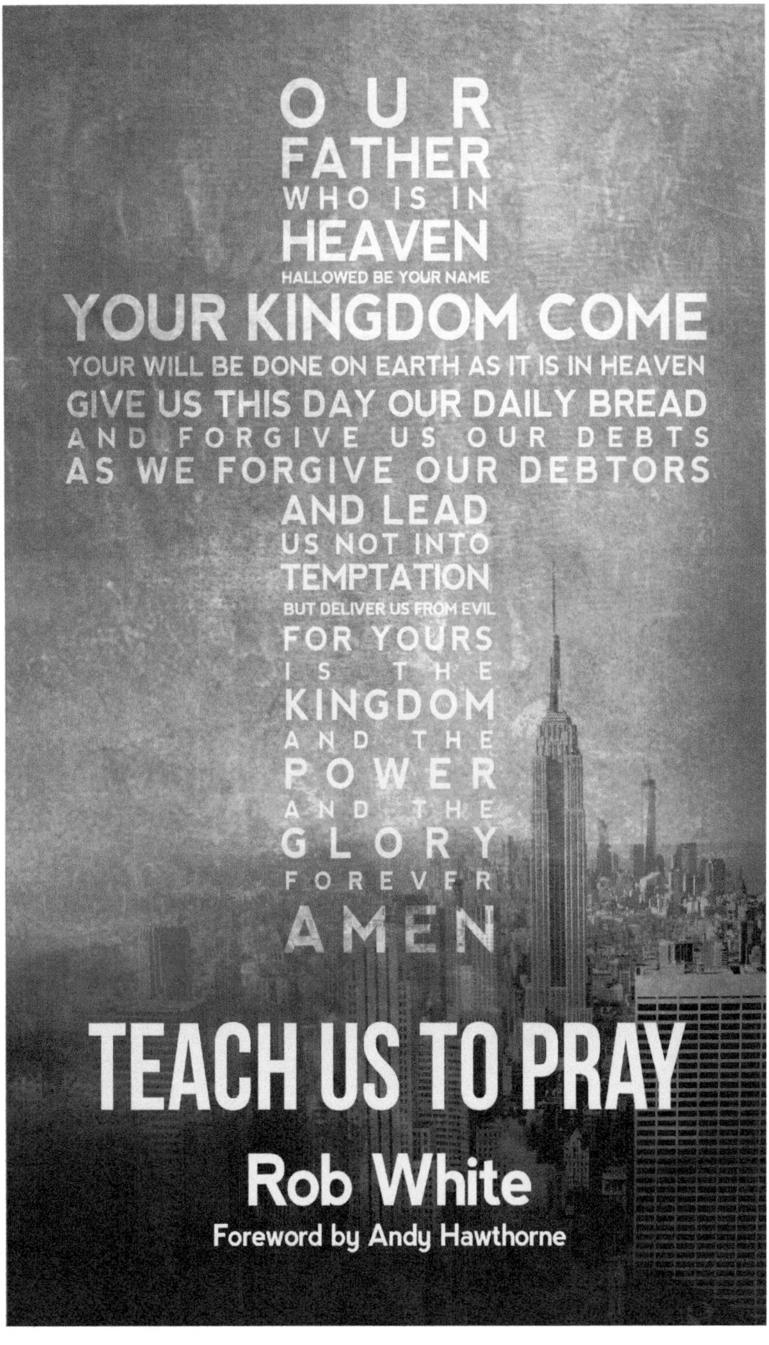
OUR
FATHER
WHO IS IN
HEAVEN
HALLOWED BE YOUR NAME
YOUR KINGDOM COME
YOUR WILL BE DONE ON EARTH AS IT IS IN HEAVEN
GIVE US THIS DAY OUR DAILY BREAD
AND FORGIVE US OUR DEBTS
AS WE FORGIVE OUR DEBTORS
AND LEAD
US NOT INTO
TEMPTATION
BUT DELIVER US FROM EVIL
FOR YOURS
IS THE
KINGDOM
AND THE
POWER
AND THE
GLORY
FOREVER
AMEN
TEACH US TO PRAY
Rob White
Foreword by Andy Hawthorne

COMING OUT
GOLD

A Quest for Sexual Purity

ROB JOY

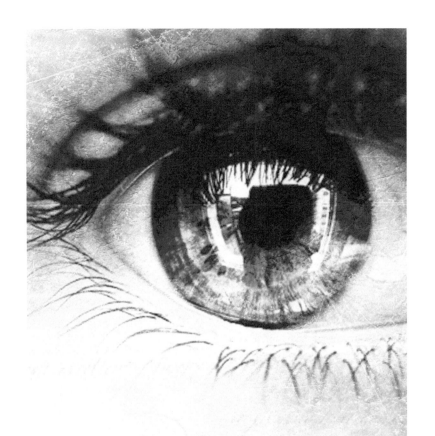

STILL EMILY

Seeing rainbows in the silence

A MEMOIR BY
EMILY OWEN

Failing Intelligently

Intelligently

Facing and Learning
from the Impact of Failure

CARIS GRIMES

MARK & CHERITH STIBBE

Restoring

THE

FALLEN

Creating safe spaces for those who fail

THIS

IS

How to see
the Kingdom of Heaven
in everyday living

THAT

Martin J Young

A True Life Story
of Living with Faith and Locked-In Syndrome

PRESSED
but not
CRUSHED

Andrew Davies
Barbara Davies and Emma Davies